WROTE FOR LUCK

Wrote for Luck
Selected Lyrics

SHAUN RYDER

FABER & FABER

This edition first published in the UK in 2019 by
Faber & Faber Ltd
Bloomsbury House
74–77 Great Russell Street
London WC1B 3DA

First published in the USA in 2019

Typeset by Hamish Ironside
Printed in the UK by TJ International Ltd, Padstow, Cornwall

A CIP record for this book is available from the British Library

ISBN 978-0-571-33093-5

MIX
Paper from
responsible sources
FSC
www.fsc.org   FSC® C013056

10 9 8 7 6 5 4 3 2 1

Contents

[vi]

Preface

I was a bit unsure when I was originally asked to do a book of my collected lyrics. I've never put myself forward as an anguished wordsmith. Where I come from you don't walk around telling everyone you're a poet when you're growing up. I never even set out to be a lyricist originally. We just wanted to start a band, and I had to start writing lyrics by default because I became the frontman of Happy Mondays, and none of the others showed any real interest in the words.

So I never for a minute saw myself as one of those tortured artists, pouring his heart out. I was a postie before the band took off, and that was torture, trust me . . . getting up at 4 a.m. and having to walk miles on your round and getting attacked by dogs. Once you've done that, you can hardly say being in a band, going on tour and seeing the world is torture.

Whatever pressure I did feel as a frontman, I used heroin to cope with it. That was my coping mechanism for a long time. So I didn't need to wear my heart on my sleeve like fucking Morrissey. That worked for him and good on him, but I'm not Morrissey and never will be, and never wanted to be. Not for a minute. I wanted to find my voice as Shaun Ryder.

I've never really read anyone else's lyrics for inspiration. I would listen out for lyrics in songs, but you know how it is, no matter how much you think you've heard the words correctly, when you see them written down you realise you've been singing the wrong fucking words for twenty-five years. I do have a bit of attention deficit disorder as well, so I have to try really hard to concentrate and focus if I'm listening to lyrics. Otherwise I'll find myself drifting off and following the bass line instead.

Very few of my songs are about one single thing. Most of them are a collection of different incidents or scenes. I write in pictures. I will get a scene in my head and I'm just painting the picture of that story. It's almost like I've got a mad cartoon running through my head and the lyrics are oddball captions describing what is happening in each frame that's in my head.

When the Mondays started, we knew there was nobody out there in the music business like us. There was no one coming from the same place as us, who lived the same lifestyle as us, or who looked like us. I remember a couple of industry people coming up from London in the mid-'80s saying stuff like, 'You need to get an image. Look at Boy George, he's got an image', and we'd be like, 'This is us, this is our image.' But they totally didn't get it. I mean, imagine telling Bez he should be dressing like Boy George, for fuck's sake. We knew we didn't want the music to sounds like anyone else, and I also wanted to find my own voice. I wanted to sound like Shaun William Ryder.

The music industry and the media are always trying to res-urrect old scenes, like mods are coming back, or something like that. So when something that is really new comes along it takes them a good few years to catch up. Not only did we know there wasn't anyone like us in the industry, we also knew that there were a lot of people out there, on the estates, in the pubs, in the clubs and down the Arndale centres or at the match, that would get us. We knew we didn't sound like any-one else, and we made sure of that. We wanted to be original, but we didn't want to be some left-field band only playing to a handful of blokes on a Thursday night in some shit venue, or a student band that never gets covered outside the *NME*. We wanted to be big and we wanted people to hear our music. We wanted to be on *Top of the Pops*.

If I was interviewed back in the day, depending on what mood I was in, I might say a song was about something more specific, about this or that, when it wasn't really. Sometimes the songs were a little more abstract or surreal, just words that sounded good and created an image in my brain when I was stringing them together. Half the time I was more concerned with how the words sounded than with what they actually meant. I actually used to change the words quite a lot, when we were writing songs and first rehearsing them and playing them. I would sing slightly different lyrics each night and what ended up on record was only the version that I sang that day.

With Happy Mondays, the way we wrote songs changed over the years. At first, a lot of the songs would come out of jamming in rehearsals and studios. Quite often the band would get into a loop, possibly because they were off their tits, or sometimes because they knew how to start a song and get into a groove, but then couldn't finish it, and I would just freestyle over the top, and a song would emerge from the best bits of that process. Later, with the acid house influence and with different remixers and producers like Paul Oakenfold, we started working more around beats in the studio. Then on the last Mondays album, the whole process collapsed, and I struggled to write anything to the music they were coming up with, which really showed.

After the Mondays finished and I started Black Grape, the writing process changed again, as I was bouncing off Kermit and it was really refreshing to have someone else to trade with lyrically, and I think you can tell that when you listen to the tunes now. Listen to the first Black Grape album and I sound completely re-energised, compared to the last Mondays album, on which you can tell I'm lacking enthusiasm and inspiration.

I didn't listen to a lot of these songs for twenty years after we recorded them, as I was always one for looking forward, rather than backward. But a few years ago I was sent a remastered copy of *Bummed* and I sat down and listened to it and I thought, 'That's fucking great!' . . . and as we've toured them over the last few years, as Happy Mondays and Black Grape, I've actually begun to appreciate them a lot more.

I still wouldn't call myself a poet though.

Shaun William Ryder

Editor's Note

> One day he was admiring his reflection, in his favourite
>   mirror
> When he realised all too clearly, what a freakin' old
>   beasty man he was

Factory boss Tony Wilson famously once claimed that Shaun
Ryder's lyrics were up there with W. B. Yeats's, although
Wilson was never short of bullish Mancunian bravado, shy
of talking up his various charges, or insisting rock 'n' roll or
acid house was deserving of at least the same level of deference
afforded to so-called high culture, if not more so.

Shaun Ryder and Happy Mondays always did sound
unique, with their innate ability to soak up disparate influ-
ences from the '60s to the '90s, from Salford to Chicago, from
Ibiza to Wigan Pier, but remould it into something completely
their own. And they still sound like nobody else, which is an
all-too-rare achievement. When the Mondays crashed and
burned, many wrote Ryder off as a burnt-out drug addict and
a lost cause, but against the odds he proved them all wrong
with one of the most remarkable comebacks in recent music
history, creating a new band, Black Grape, who stood out as a
beacon of refreshing originality in a world dominated by the
retro dad-rock of Britpop. The fact that Shaun William Ryder
was the only constant in both groups speaks volumes. He may
not have played a note on any instrument, but he was a mav-
erick magpie, a madcap lyricist and instinctive alchemist who
was the catalyst for some incredible, groundbreaking records.

When the bulk of these songs were written and released,
Shaun Ryder was caught in the eye of the storm, submerged
in the subterranean world of a city that was on the cusp of a
renaissance, awash with new drugs and a music scene which

felt revolutionary, surrounded by a cast of scallies, chancers, dreamers, drug dealers and users, ne'er-do-wells and street gangsters. And that was just his band and entourage. Day-to-day life was far more fantastical and intoxicating than anything he could concoct, so he wrote about what he saw around him, painting jagged cartoon pictures and kaleidoscopic vignettes of a world of intoxicated individuals that was itself utterly intoxicating – a world of twenty-four-hour party people, dirty drug deals, graphic sex, petty crime and violence, which swung between euphoric highs and mind-numbing lows. He had an innate astuteness to capture what was going on around him, and could sum up the essence of a character in an offbeat line that would resonate with many people in a way which meant the songs hit home. That he managed to do this through the haze of a heavy drug use is all the more remarkable.

His lyrics are inhabited by a mixed cast of the usual suspects, including the band and their hangers on, groupies and girlfriends, along with thinly veiled caricatures of himself that are more often self-deprecating than self-aggrandising. Tina Weymouth of Talking Heads (who produced the last Mondays album) once said of Shaun and the band: 'I grew up in New York in the seventies, and I've seen a lot of people who live life on the edge, but I've never before seen a group of people who had no idea where the edge is.'

Shaun's lyrics were eclectic, marrying oddball characters with chants from the dancefloor, friends' nicknames and in-joke catchphrases with popular culture, film and literary references, all retold through his own prism. They are a trapdoor to a surreal, violent, joyous, profane underworld where normal rules don't apply, with the best and worst drugs and all-night bacchanalian parties, but always with a warning of an undercurrent of violence and the comedown that follows any euphoric high. A world of drug dealers and drug takers, bent coppers and postmen on the make, loose women and even looser men, hallucinations and sexually transmitted diseases, living on the breadline waiting days for the dole check, needles and tin foil, Rizlas and hot knives, the good, the bad and the ugly of every drug experience – from the deep anaesthetising comfort blanket of heroin to the exhilarating euphoric rush of ecstasy, the manic rush of speed to the madness of tramazi parties. Even in the halcyon days, Shaun's lyrics were never totally euphoric; they remained littered with real-life tales of deaths and drug causalities, bridges burned and lessons unlearned. Throughout this psychedelic ethnography he was never afraid to be self-deprecating, declaring, 'I don't have a decent bone in me, what you see is what you get.'

What's remarkable, a quarter of a century on, is how Shaun Ryder's lyrics, like the music, still have an utterly unique voice. He ordered a line, and you formed a queue. He used to speak the truth, but now he's clever.

Luke Bainbridge

WROTE FOR LUCK

Kuff Dam

If you've got to be told by someone then it's got to be me
And that's not made from cheese and it doesn't get you free
So now you're wising up to know you need a job
Don't bite, don't bite, don't bite out in here
It's been nice wasting time, it's not worth your while

Blow on, go on, blow on, go up and spill it all out
And if we have to be shown by someone then it won't be you
You see that Jesus is a cunt, and never helped you with a
    thing that you do, or you done
It won't be long, it won't be long, to get rid of your furry
    tongue
It's going in, out, it's going in, out

Blow on, go on, blow on, go on, and stroke a left side
Go on, blow on, go on, blow on, and stroke a right side
You're biting into the root, you're smoking pot to the wall
Blow on, go on, blow on, go on and take it full blown
Kuff Dam, Dam Kuff
Kuff Dam, Dam Kuff

*We were signed to Factory so early on in our career that we
were thrown into the recording studio before we were really
ready. Some of our early recordings shouldn't have made it on
to vinyl really. 'Kuff Dam' and 'Tart Tart' were the first tracks
we managed to record in the studio that I felt truly captured
the sense and the potential of the Mondays. It was definitely
the first time that I felt I was beginning to find my voice, and
beginning to sound like me, rather than trying to be something
else.*

[3]

The title 'Kuff Dam' was taken from a porno movie called Mad Fuck, but spelt backwards. It's me starting to find my voice and rhythm, realising that is more important than trying to tell a complete story in a song.

You see that Jesus is a cunt, and never helped you with a
    thing that you do, or you done

I wouldn't dream of using a lyric like that now, but I simply didn't care back then. Even though I came from a really strong Catholic background, my mam has never said anything about any of the lyrics. Even if she picked up on them, she would just shrug and let it wash over her.

Tart Tart

When If came out of the lock-up
He said I'm looking for something better
And he made his shock announcement
And backed off, backed down, backed off

And then he got up off the floor
He said I'm wealthy enough, not to do this no more
And he made it all known
With his hands held up, palm out

And she said don't know if I should
'Cause I worry too much about the tests on the blood
And at first it was a 'yes', and then a 'no', then a 'yes'

And maggot sleeps on his desk
He wears a sleeping bag as his vest
And he's getting too bothered
About the spots on his chest, chest, chest

Now TT, she laid it on
And a few days later she's gone
So it's back to the womb
To get drowned, drowned, drowned, drowned warm

*'Tart Tart' was named after a woman that me and Bez knew
called Dinah, from Chorlton, who we affectionately nicknamed 'Tart Tart'. She was quite a bit older than us, well into
her thirties when we met her, when we were just in our early
twenties. She'd been around the block and had been a bit of a
groupie in the late '60s, but was still around and dealing speed*

*in the '80s when we met her. She would always be there when
we played the Boardwalk in the early days.*

Now TT, she laid it on
And a few days later she's gone

*Tart Tart took a bit of a shine to me and Bez, and was very
good to us, letting us crash at her flat when we needed to and
laying speed on tick for us. Then one day a roadie we knew
called Martin Smith, who also used to score whizz off her,
popped round to her flat and there was no answer. He sus-
pected something was up, so broke in and found her body.
Poor Tart Tart had just had a brain haemorrhage and died.*

So it's back to the womb
To get drowned, drowned, drowned, drowned warm

*This is a reference to heroin, and that warm feeling of escap-
ism it gives you, that is like returning to the womb.*

And she said don't know if I should
'Cause I worry too much about the tests on the blood
And at first it was a 'yes', and then a 'no', then a 'yes'

*The rest of the lyrics aren't about Tart Tart. This was written
around that time in the early to mid-'80s that AIDS was all
over the news, but most people were still pretty ill-informed
about it, and so some people were really paranoid about it.*

And he's getting too bothered
About the spots on his chest, chest, chest

*This is about our Paul, he was one of those who was always
paranoid about catching AIDS, he'd come in to rehearsal and
go 'Look at these spots on my chest, fucking hell, what do you
think it is?'*

[6]

'Enery

Spread your germ, spread your germ
Spread your germ, spread your germ, pass your germ
Spread your germ, pass your germ
Spread your bug

It's no national secret
You can't stop and wait here
Getting the attention that it wants
Give it the attention which it needs
A strong, strong, strong, strong, strong medicine
Won't put you right this time

Spread your germ, spread your germ
Bring your bug, bring your germs, pass your bug

Give it the affection it should have
Give it the attention which it needs

The international bus
Has come to pick up
You and Horse
It's not that food
That you get from your tin
Your body's looking
Too thin

You pass your bug, pass your bug
Pass your bug, spread your bug
Spread your germs

Spread your germs
Pass your bug

"Enery' is just about sexually transmitted diseases. At the time I wrote that, I was living with Bez and our Paul were crashing at my flat and there were a lot of sexually transmitted diseases passed on around our extended group. There were a number of girls we hung about with at this time, who weren't necessarily groupies, but being so young and living the sort of lifestyles we were, almost everyone ends up shagging each other.

Weekends

You think you're better than the rest of us by a million miles
And I know we're okay, not in good shape but you'll have
to do
We thought we saw you from behind, so you got slapped on
your shoulder
Back attack
You didn't mind you just laughed youse way over there

Let's get out of here, everybody in here, they all look like
you do
Let's get out of here, everybody in here they all grin like you
And we both steaming, smiling happy faces
But when you turn away, you get daggers in your back

Hey let's get out of this place, everybody in here they all look
like you
Hey let's get out of here, everybody in this place they all grin
like you do
Oh gotta get out, gotta get out, gotta get out, gotta get out
of here
Out of here

'Weekends' was based on my experiences of going out in
Manchester, to horrible old school bars and clubs in the mid-
1980s, before acid house hit and changed everything. Places
like Oscars and Rotters, that were just awful cattle markets for
gangs of lads and girls. Every town or city had places like that.

Let's get out of here, everybody in here, they all look
    like you do
Let's get out of here, everybody in here they all grin
    like you

In that period just before acid house hit, people were still dressing up to go out rather than dressing down. When 17 and 18-year-olds couldn't get in anywhere if they weren't wearing a pair of proper shoes and a pair of smart pants. I hated it. They were just awful places full of small town knobheads who drank too much and there would always be a fight, and some-one might get glassed. One of the many reasons the Haçienda was such a revelation when it opened, was it was the complete antithesis to that, especially in the early days before those gangs of lads in shiny shirts got on to it.

Eventually, of course, those dicks did start turning up.
They always do, eventually.

24 Hour Party People

How old are you? Are you old enough?
Should you be in here watching that?
And how old are you? Are you owning up?
Should you be in here with?
Twenty-four hour party people
Plastic face carnt smile the white out
With the twenty-four hour party people
Plastic face can't smile the white out
You cannot beat 'em
So why don't you join in?
You cannot beat 'em
So why don't you join in with?
Twenty-four hour party people
Plastic face carnt smile the white out
With the twenty-four hour party people
Plastic face carnt smile the white out
I can see you through the door
You been chewing bread and water
And there's a grudge on you
You know you not ought to have
You've been running around the racetrack
You've been running around the ragetrack
Put that mudder to bed, to bed
Put that mudder to bed
With the twenty-four hour party people
Plastic face carnt smile a white out
'Cause I have to wait for you to conduct
Press the pause of the self-destruct
With the twenty-four hour party people
Plastic face carnt smile the white out
With the twenty-four hour party people

Now better, you're the white out
I need full-time, I don't need part-time
I need 1, 2, 3, 4, 5, 6, 7, 3, 6, 5 all the time
I need 1, 2, 3, 4, 5, 6, 7 third time
I don't need a part-time, I need a 3, 6, 5
Oh, no days off
Twenty-four hour party people
Plastic face carnt smile the white out
I need 1, 2, 3, 4, 5, 6, 7, 3, 6, 5 all the time
I need 1, 2, 3, 4, 5, 6, 7 third time
I don't need a part-time, I mean 3, 6, 5
No days off

By the time of '24 Hour Party People' I had really begun to find my voice, and I was writing about our lives and the things that were happening around me and to me, rather than trying to write about what I thought you should write about. Our mate Minny used to call me and our kid 'the 24-hour party people', because that was the life we were living, just living for the day and the party; never thinking about tomorrow. We had a bright yellow car at the time, which was nicknamed 'The Egg', which there's another Mondays song named after. People would say, 'Here come the 24-hour party people in the Egg'.

You've been running around the racetrack
You've been running around the ragetrack

Ecstasy still hadn't hit Manchester, but there was a lot of amphetamines around at the time, and you could look like you were running when you were dancing if you were really racing on speed. Amphetamines could also get you absolutely raging, so that's just a simple play on words.

Put that mudder to bed, to bed
Put that mudder to bed

There would always be someone who was a bit too wired, who would start doing everyone's heads in, and everyone would be like, someone 'Put that mudder to bed', 'mudder' meaning motherfucker.

With the twenty-four hour party people
Plastic face carnt smile a white out

I think it was the same mate Minny who came out with that as well, one time when we were all so wired that we couldn't really smile; when you get really wired you would get this fixed grin on your face, with gritted teeth, like you've almost got lockjaw. He just popped his head round the door, took one look at us and went, 'Fucking hell, twenty-four hour party people, plastic face carnt smile a white out . . .'

Country Song

Well I'm a simply city boy
With simple country tastes
Smoking wild-grown marijuana
Keeps that smile on your face
But it says so, so longer to you
But it says so, so longer

Listening to my system, just the other night
Watching my TV with the sound turned down
Checking out the late, late, late, night fight
Checking out the late, late, late, night fight

Biting off your hands
Throwing your peas and pans
Knocking you to the floor
Accusing you, you filthy whore
For more, more, more, more, more now
More, more, more, too much more

Well I'm a simply city boy
With simple country tastes
Smoking wild-grown marijuana
Keeps that smile on your face
Depending on the mood, mood, mood, mood, mood, mood
Depending on the mood, mood, mood, mood, mood, mood

Better up your house for sale, the Indians are coming
Better up your house for sale, the Indians are coming
Redneck, gotta lot of redneck in ya
Redneck, gotta lot of redneck in ya

Better up your house for sale, the Indians are coming
Better up your house for sale, the Indians are coming
Redneck, gotta lot of redneck in ya

Before Bummed, *we knew the music we wanted to play in our heads, but we hadn't necessarily worked out how to get it out, how to create the sounds we had in our heads – both the band as musicians and me as a songwriter. By the time we came to write and record Bummed, our second album, we had been rehearsing in the basement of the Boardwalk for a while and were really getting it down as a band. So we decided to try and do a Salford version of a country song. It was originally called 'Some Cunt from Preston', which was our slang for country and western.*

Moving in With

You've got two bent pigs in the crash downstairs below
Chewing at the door, I said, 'Why you so slow?'
Got a schizophrenic acquaintance patient with no place
    to go
Stuck with his dick through my window

We're moving in, on, with you
You're moving in, on, me and

Henny Penny, Cocky Locky, Goosey Loosey, Turkey Lurkey,
    Ducky Lucky, Chicken Licken
It seems we're all on the move when the sound's falling in
It seems we're all on the move when the sound's falling in
I'd say they're all on the move, when the sky's coming in

You got four muddy pigs in the flat downstairs below
Chomping at the door, he say, 'Why you so slow?'
Got a schizophrenic acquaintance patient with no place
    to go
Stuck with his dick through my Afghani window

We're moving in, on, with you
You're moving in, on, me and

Henny Penny, Cocky Locky, Goosey Loosey, Turkey Lurkey,
    Chicken Licken, Ducky Lucky
I'd say we're all on the move when the sound's falling in
I'd say we're all on the move when the sound's falling in
I'd say they're all on the move when the door's coming in

I like a bit of a cavort, old ladies and important inhabitants

This song is all about the gaff that I was living in at the time, in Boothsdown in Salford. It was 1987, just as the E first arrived on the scene. Me and my girlfriend lived there at first, then when we split up it ended up being me, Bez and our kid, and it was a madhouse. The door to the flat was broken for a start, because we were always forgetting our keys, so it was basically an open house, and all these mad heads would turn up at all times of the day and night. I also used to use it as a stash house, because we were selling drugs at the time, so I had all sorts hidden in the loft, 8 bars, acid, smack and then the E when it arrived. We had kids from Moss Side coming over bringing us pounds of weed to knock out.

You've got two bent pigs in the crash downstairs below
Chewing at the door, I said, 'Why you so slow?'

'Crash' just means a crash pad, which is what that gaff was, it was hardly home sweet home, it was just a crash pad. The two bent pigs were two coppers who we used to serve up. They would come round and buy all sorts from us – speed, weed and even smack sometimes. They just used to pull up in their panda car and buy it off us.

Got a schizophrenic acquaintance patient with no place to go
Stuck with his dick through my window

A huge black kid called Paul, who had gone to school with Bez, was always coming round to the gaff when we moved in. He was schizophrenic, due to a breakdown caused by drugs. He had been sectioned and when he came out he started dressing in these huge traditional African gowns, and would walk around with a live kitten on each shoulder. We used to let him in at first, but he was a big lump of a lad, and started to try and intimidate people and there was no way we were having that, so we told him he couldn't come round anymore.

'My Afghani window' is a reference to Afghani black, the type of weed we were smoking and selling at the moment, which had a really strong smell, so you could smell it a mile off if you were just passing the window.

Henny Penny, Cocky Locky, Goosey Loosey, Turkey Lurkey, Ducky Lucky, Chicky Licken

That is lifted from the old folk tale, but I'm using it to refer to our Paul, Bez and all the crowd who used to hang around that gaff. Back then we would hardly ever use someone's real name, everyone had about four nicknames, which would come in handy if you were involved in a drug deal or something.

Mad Cyril

We've been courteous
I like that, turn it up, I like that, turn it up
It was Mad Cyril, It was Mad Cyril
I like that, turn it up

Although our music and our drugs stay the same
Although our music and our interests are the same
We've been together, fuckers from the well
We've smoked together and we slipped down in hell

Hell, wants me
Hell, wants you back

Although our music and our drugs stay the same
Although our interests and our music stayed the same
We've went together, druggers from the well
We've smoked together and we slipped down in hell

Hell, needs me
Hell, wants me, oh

Are you ready? Let's go
Are you ready?

Give me, give me, give me
Give me, give me, give me a break
Give me, give me, give me
Give me, give me, give me a break

Hell, fuck just about everything allowed
Hell, fuck about everything

Although our music and our drugs stayed the same
Although our interests and our music stayed the same
We went together, druggers from the well
We've smoked together and we slipped down in hell

Put the frighteners on the flash little twerp
Let's have a look, let's have a look, excuse me
But come in, take a look, take a look

It's a right piss hole, long hair, beatniks
Druggers, freeloaders, tsk, freeloaders
I need a bohemian atmosphere
I like that, turn it up

'Mad Cyril' was a character from Performance, which was a huge film for us back in the mid-'80s. People forget now, when you've got Netflix and YouTube, and thousands of films to watch at the press of a button, but back then you would only have a handful of videos in your house. You'd have half a dozen films that were your favourites and you'd watch them over and over and over again, especially when you were stoned. We must have watched Performance hundreds of times, off our boxes, almost wearing the tape out. It wasn't an easy film to get hold of back then, so not everyone knew it, but we loved it and there's references to it all over Bummed, our second album.

Fat Lady Wrestlers

I just got back from a year in the sack
It must've been something I'm eating
I just got back from a year away
It's down to something you're drinking

You've been seen, you've been seen, you've been seen,
    you've been seen, you've been seen, you've been seen,
    you've been seen
You've been seen, you've been seen, you've been seen,
    you've been seen, you've been seen, you've been seen,
    you've been seen
You've been with fat lady wrestlers
And Germans in trenches,
And teachers who speak to themself
Snide sneak corner, and baby beat a pauper,
Peasants who eat from the road

I've just got back from a year away
It must've been something I'm drinking somewhere
I just got back from a year in the sack
It's down to something you're eating

You did work, you did work, you did work, you did work,
    you did work,
you did work, you did work
You did work, you did work, you did work, you did work,
    you did work,
you did work, you did work

You did it with fat lady wrestlers
And Germans in trenches
And teachers who eat on their own, sometime
Snide sneak corner, and baby beats a pauper
And gypos who steal from their own

I just got back from a year away
It must've been something I'm drinking somewhere
Just got back from a year in the sack
Did you suss the clowns that you're meetin'?

You did work, you did work, you did work, you did work,
    you did work,
you did work, you did work
You did work, you did work, you did work, you did work,
    you did work,
you did work, you did work

'Fat Lady Wrestlers' is another song that kind of sums up the life we were living then. We were very much living like crazy hustlers, from day to day; we weren't living a normal existence in any way. We weren't really making any money from music yet, so we were still doing hustles and sneaks everywhere to make a living.

I'd just got back from a year away in Amsterdam, which is what I refer to at the start of the song. 'You've been seen, you've been seen' is just a reference to both trying to get away with what you were up to at times, and also clocking someone else, one of your pals, up to something. You've been seen.

Halfway through the writing of these songs the E arrived, and we were the first on it in Manchester. That changed everything, your outlook, your music, the way you looked, the way you acted, the way you danced . . . everything. When we went to record the album in Driffield, with a few of our pals,

Manchester was dry, because we had all the E in Driffield. We used to live on it at first, literally, we were eating if every day. We took 200 pills to Driffield and ran out after a few days. So Bummed *is an ecstasy album really.*

Performance

One day he was admiring his reflection in his favourite
    mirror
When he realised all too clearly what a freakin' old beasty
    man he was
Who is? You is, you is now, son
I took to hiding, I took to hiding, I took to hiding, hiding
    strange things
I took to dribbling, I took to dribbling down my front
I starting running, I starting running on the spot
Picked ya picture, now I'm gonna eat ya
Picked ya picture, now I'm gonna eat ya
We're all food, you're cake
We're all the food, your weirdos' cream
Quick, quick, fast, fast, quick, quick, fast, fast
I took to dribbling, I took to dribbling down my front
You took to hiding, you took to hiding strange things
One day she was touching her reflection, in her favourite
    mirror
when she realised all too clearly, what a freakin' old weirdo
    she was
Who was? She was, she is
Fast, fast, quick, quick, quick, quick, fast, fast
She took to hiding, she took to hiding strange things
I took to dribbling, I took to dribbling down my front

*We've played some of these songs recently live with the Mondays
for the first time in 25 years, and when I sing them now it's
with real fondness. We were just kids really, and they were just
crazy days. I also enjoy playing them because I don't think we
appreciated how good they were at the time.*

We were always pushing ourselves, so nothing was ever quite good enough back then. I didn't hear some of these songs for 20 years, until I was sent a remastered version of Bummed *that was coming out, and I sat down and listened to it and thought, 'That's fucking great!'*

Obviously the title if this song is another nod to the film Performance, *which we were obsessed with at the time.*

I took to hiding, I took to hiding, hiding strange things
You took to hiding, you took to hiding, hiding strange
    things

This is another reference to the gaff I had in Boothsdown with Bez and our Paul that is mentioned in 'Moving in With'. You had to hide whatever you had when you were living there – drugs, money, even your clothes – or they would be gone when you woke up. Literally. It was first up, best dressed in that gaff. You had to stash your decent stuff, otherwise one of the others would nick it.

I took to dribbling, I took to dribbling down
    my front
I starting running, I starting running on the spot

This is a drugs reference. Bez could be off his tits and he would be dribbling, dribbling down his front. Then, if you have taken speed or ecstasy, which was just arriving, that's how people would dance, especially Bez, as if they were running on the spot.

One day she was touching her reflection, in her
    favourite mirror
when she realised all too clearly, what a freakin' old
    weirdo she was

This is just me flipping the first chorus so instead of being about me, it's about Suzy, my girlfriend at the time, as me and her were like a couple of misfits on the E scene.

Brain Dead

You're rendering that scaffolding dangerous!

Grass-eyed, slashed-eyed, brain-dead fucker
Rips off himself, steals from his brother,
Loathed by everyone, but loved by his mother

It not the hip or the ship, that gets you caught
No one likes to feel that they've been bought
Why then?
Should you do it again and again and again?

He's a wise guy, when guy, don't like my eye spy
Always a snide try, never a clean guy
Loathed by everyone, but loved by his mother

Give you a calls
For the, thing upstairs
She take him his night-time brown and flask
Sews up his night-time brown and mask
You bleed in my eye
You bleed in my eye
White track

Grass-eyed, slashed-eyed, brain-dead fuck-up
Rips off himself, and steals from his brother
Loathed by everyone, but loved by his mother
(Kiss kiss)

Why then?
Should you do it again and again and again?
Why then?
Do you do it again and again and again?

Wrote for Luck

I wrote for luck, they sent me you
I sent for juice, you give me poison
I order a line, you form a queue
You're trying so hard, there's nothing else you can do
Well not much, I've not been trained
I can sit and stand, beg and roll over
And I don't read, I just guess
There's more than one sign, but it's getting less
And you were wet, but you're getting drier
You used to speak the truth, but now you're liar
You used to speak the truth, but now you're clever

And I wrote for luck, they sent me you
And I sent for juice, you give me poison
I order a line, you form a queue
You're trying so hard, there's nothing else you can do
And you were wet, but you're getting drier
You used to speak the truth, but now you're clever
You used to speak the truth, but now you're clever
And when it's hot, you start to melt
'Cause you're not made of cheese, you're made of chocolate
And when it cold, you turn to crack
And keep on piling out, not pulling back

I love 'Wrote For Luck', but it was never quite finished in my opinion. I just felt it needed a tiny bit more work. But it was a big step up wise in terms of structure. For a long time it was the song that we used to finish our gigs with. It's another one of those songs that really sums up what life was like for me and the band at that time. We were still having to do various snide things to make a living sometimes.

I wrote for luck, they sent me you

Everyone needs a bit of luck sometimes. We could have been in the rehearsal room trying to come up with a song and wishing for some inspiration, or I might have been skint and needing a bit of luck. Other people in a dire situation might look to God, and praying is only asking for luck in a way isn't it?

It's also a reference to the E in a way, because that changed everything for us. We suddenly had money, 'cause we were the first to get on it, so we were selling it, but it also changed our lifestyle and changed the music. So I wrote for luck and they sent me E, in a way.

I sent for juice, you give me poison

This is a reference to the bad drugs that could be knocking around at time, when someone has ripped you off in a drug deal.

You try and think hard, there's nothing else you can do,
Well not much, I've not been trained

I'd come out of school at 14 and didn't have any qualifications. I'd been a postman for a bit and there was no way I was going back to that, or going to work in Tesco or something, so what else was I going to do apart from be in a band or sell drugs?

I don't read, I just guess
There's more than one sign, but it's getting less

I also left school without knowing my alphabet, and I only finally got round to learning it on tour with the Mondays shortly after we took off. Our manager Nathan McGough turned round to us and said the band had made our first million, and for some reason that made me think, 'I suppose I better learn my fucking alphabet now'.

You used to speak the truth, but now you're liar
You used to speak the truth, but now you're clever

That's a self-reference to me and Bez and our public image. From the start, me and Bez quickly realised that if we played up to the bad boy image then the press and the public would lap it up. The press loved it as we always gave them great, outrageous quotes, but we knew exactly what we were doing. We knew it was all great fuel for the Happy Mondays myth. Tony Wilson always used to say to us, 'Never let the truth get in the way of a good story.' Most other people in the music industry wanted to keep any mention of drugs out of the public eye, but we didn't give a fuck. We would happily talk about drugs to any journalists, and wouldn't even think twice about doing drugs in front of them. The other plus point of that is no one could ever do a number on us, because we'd been upfront about everything from day one. There were no skeletons in my closet, they were all on full display.

You were wet, but you're getting drier

That's lifted from the David Essex film Stardust. *Adam Faith visits him in a castle and says to him, 'You're wet', and he says, 'Yeah, but I'm getting drier'.*
When we were recording 'Wrote For Luck' and Bummed, *one of our lads turned up back from Ibiza and he had bought all Oakenfold's records off him at the end of the summer. So he turned up at the studio and we were playing all these tunes in between recording. Factory wanted Vince Clarke from Erasure to remix 'Wrote For Luck' for a single, but I said let's get Paul Oakenfold to do a remix as well. I much preferred the Oakenfold remix as did any of the kids who were out there on the acid house scene and knew what the score was. But Factory insisted the Vince Clarke mix went on the A-side, as he had four records in the charts at the time and was a bigger name,*

and stuck Oakey's remix on the B-side. But I was proved right, as all the DJs wanted to play was the Oakey mix. But it worked out in the end, as that persuaded Factory to let Oakey and Steve Osborne produce our next album, Pills 'n' Thrills and Bellyaches.

Bring a Friend

Upped and leave my home
Left a message on the answerin' phone
You said whipped through your cash
Through a porno moustache
Bought a kipper tie and a ticket to fly
Now I'm walking with a swagger
Going deep down with my dagger
'Scene one . . . take one'
Clio and her sister Rio, were watching through the keyhole
Make your way in, rub up your skin
Let the scene begin, woah

Well I might be the honky
But I'm hung like a donkey
So I'm tied to a bed, with a pussy on my head
Surrounded by ugly girls
There's no rust on me
I don't thrust for free
You can see me on page 1 to 103
Now the rules of my occupation
I say 'yes' in every situation
You keep an undone fly
Let your nosebag dry
So come on in
Grease up the skin
Make me seed again
Bring a friend

Don't need no concentration
My pelvis is my inspiration
And you run out to work and my tie needs a jerk
I live in a house that's made out of dirt
Clio and her sister Rio
We're rubbin' through the keyhole
They were makin' loud grunts with their three little cunts
And the action started again
So come on in
Grease up your skin
Make a scene begin

A lot of the lyrics from 'Bring a Friend' are taken from an incident when I was busted coming back from Amsterdam in the early '80s with a load of weed and some porn. I was only about 21 at the time, and they took everything off me, and this big old customs officer sat in front of me going through this porn magazine and circling things she thought were too hardcore, (which is also referenced in 'Holiday' on Pills 'n' Thrills and Bellyaches*). They confiscated the magazine but certain things from the magazine had stuck with me for some reason. It had that late '70s Dutch porn feel, and reminded me of* Performance *a bit, as if it could be a dream scene that Mick Jagger had in the film. So 'Bring a Friend' is basically me describing that dream sequence. 'Clio and her sister Rio' were the stars of that magazine and there was a guy with a kipper tie and a porno moustache. The line 'They were makin' loud grunts with their three little cunts' is also lifted from the magazine.*

Do It Better

On one, in one, did one, do one, did one, have one, in one,
   have one
Come on, have one, did one, do one, good one, in one,
   have one

Swapped the dog for a cold, cold ride
It was deformed on the in, but deformed on the outside
Stuck a piece of crack in a butcher's hand
Remind me to give me my cat back
Don't purchase me 'cause I won't work
I gave away my oil and the seeds in my boots
There was a boom in the room when the papers marched in
He pulls himself together and sat down

Mislaid the dog for a dumb old ride
She was dumber on the in, deformed on the outside
Stuck a piece of crack in a good girl's hand
Demanded she give me my love back
Took my path with a touch of life
'Cause there's hills you don't take and roads you can't climb
There was a boom in the room as the snidey snide in
They snide themselves together and snide down

On one, in one, did one, do one, did one, did one, have one
In one, have one, have two, have three, have one, have one
In one, do one, do it one better

Good, good, good, good, good, good, good, good, good,
   good, good, good
Double double good
Double double good

Good, good, good, good, good, good, good, good, good,
   good, good, good
Double double good
Double double good

On one, in one, did one, do one, did one, did one, have one
In one, have one, have two, have three, have one, have one
In one, do one, do it one better

*'Do It Better' was a real E song, and it just reminds me of the
time when the Ecstasy had just arrived in Manchester. The song
was even simply called 'E' at first, and it's also in the key of E.*

   Stuck a piece of crack in a butcher's hand
   remind me to give me my cat back

*There was a Chinese chippy near us at the time, and the own-
ers got nicked, because apparently they found a load of cats in
the freezer.*

   Don't purchase me, 'cause I won't work
   I gave away my oil and the seeds in my boots

*That was a reference to all of us being a bit lazy and stone-
heads. Don't purchase me mate; don't pick me mate, because I
won't work, I'm lazy.*

   On one, in one, did one, do one, did one, did one, have one
   In one, have one, have two, have three, have one, have one
   In one, do one, do it one better

*That's self-explanatory. It's all about the E, obviously. Every-
thing was all about the E. 'Have you got one?', 'Are you on
one?', 'Has she done one?', 'Do you want one?'*

Lazyitis

Now that one got lazyitis
And that one go it alone
And this one go 'wah wah wah wah wah wah wah wah wah'
All the way home
Now my homeboy I don't come top of the class
Got no brown tongue lickin' ass
Can't do what he's asked
Won't do what he's asked

I think I did the right thing by slipping away
And the ache that's making me ache has gone for the day
Now I'm the man that shot the boss
I pinned him down and blew his face off
I'm doing time with weirdo kind
Hustlin' and rustlin' and watchin' from behind
Now that's the man that shot the boss
He pinned him down and blew his face off
He's doing time with weirdo kind
Hustlin' and rustlin' and watchin' from behind

Now that one got lazyitis
And that one go it alone
And that one go 'wah wah wah wah wah wah wah wah wah'
All the way home
All the way home

We were aiming for an off-the-wall pop song with 'Lazyitis', although I'm not sure we quite nailed it. It was Tony Wilson's idea to bring Karl Denver in on vocals with me, and re-record it as a single. Apparently, my dad had took me to a Karl Denver gig when I was just a toddler, but I don't remember it. We obviously all knew him from his hit single 'Wimoweh', though. We shot the video underneath the Mancunian Way, and the idea was that we were all convicts, playing football in the rain in the prison yard. Quite ironic, really, because I later got nicked while trying to promote it, as I had to fly to Jersey to do some press and the customs searched me and found some empty drug bags.

Step On

You're twistin' my melon man, you know you talk so hip
  man, you're twistin' my melon man
Call the cops!

Hey rainmaker, come away from that man
You know he's gonna take away your promised land
Hey good lady he just wants what you got
You know, he'll never stop until he's taken the lot
Hey hey he hey hey

Gonna stamp out your fire, he can change your desire
Don't you know he can make you forget, you're a man
Gonna stamp out your fire, he can change your desire
Don't you know he can make you forget, you're a man,
  you're a man
Twistin' my melon man, speak so hip

Hey rainmaker he got golden plans, I tell you
You'll make a stranger in your own land
Hey good lady, he got God on his side
He got a double tongue, you never think he would lie
O lie, twistin' my melon man, twistin' my melon man

Gonna stamp out your fire, he can change your desire
Don't you know he can make you forget, you're a man
Gonna stamp out your fire, he can change your desire
Don't you know he can make you forget, you're the man,
  you're the man

He's gonna step on you again, he's gonna step on you
He's gonna step on you again, he's gonna step on you

Hey rainmaker, come away from that man
You know he's gonna take away your promised land
Hey good lady, he got God on his side
He got a double tongue, you never think he would lie

Gonna stamp out your fire, he can change your desire
Don't you know he can make you forget, you're a man
Gonna stamp out your fire, he can change your desire
Don't you know he can make you forget, you're the man,
    you're the man

Twistin' my melon man, you know you talk so hip, you're
    twistin' my melon man

I think a lot of people still think 'Step On' is a Happy Mon-days song, but it's a John Kongos cover that we made our own. At the start of 1990, we were asked to do a cover version for our American label, Elektra, for their anniversary. It was their fortieth anniversary and they wanted every Elektra band to cover a song by another Elektra band for a compilation. They sent us a tape of Elektra songs and the first or second song was 'Step On' by John Kongos. I'd never heard it before, but I could tell it would be easy for us. We really wanted to make it our own, so I added a few different lines and catchphrases and they're the ones that people remember really – 'you're twisting my melon' and 'call the cops!'

You're twistin' my melon man, you know you talk so
    hip man, you're twistin' my melon man

I'd just watched a Steve McQueen documentary called Man on the Edge, *and in it one of the big-shot producers is describ-ing when he first met McQueen and says something like, 'This cool kid came in, and you could tell he was an actor. He just looked like a cool street kid and he spoke so hip. He said to me, "You can't tell me what's what, man! You're twisting my melon, man!"' I thought, 'I'll have that – "you're twisting my melon man, you talk so hip, you know you're twisting my melon man".'*

Call the cops!

This came from a kid in the Haçienda called Bobby Gillette, who was always shouting 'Call the cops!' He'd stand in the Haçi with all our lot, off his nut, whistling and shouting, 'Call the cops! . . . We're here! The Mancs! Our firm! Our corner! . . . CALL THE COPS!!'
I knew I wanted to put a little twist on 'Step On', so I simply put those two catchphrases together and they fitted, and they ended up being the two lines that everyone remembers from the song.

Kinky Afro

Son, I'm 30, I only went with your mother 'cause she's dirty
And I don't have a decent bone in me
What you get is just what you see yeah
So I take it greedy, and all the bad piss-ugly things I feed me
I never help or give to the needy
Come on and see me

Yippy yippy aye aye eh
I had to crucify some brother today
And I don't dig what you gotta say
So come on and say it
Come on and tell me twice

I said Dad you're shabby
You run around and groove like a baggy
You're only here just out of habit
All that's mine you might as well have it
You take ten feet back and then stab it
Spray it on and tag it
So sack all the needy
I can't stand you near me
Get around here if you're asking you're feeling

Yippy yippy aye aye eh
I had to crucify somebody today
And I don't dig what you gotta say
So come on and say it
Come on and tell me twice

So sack all the needy
I can't stand to leave it
You come around here and you put both your feet in

Yippy yippy aye aye eh
I had to crucify somebody today
And I don't dig what you gotta say
So go on and say it
I had to crucify some brother today
And I don't hear what you gotta say
So come on and say it
Come on and tell me twice

'Kinky Afro' was the first song we finished for Pills 'n' Thrills
and Bellyaches, *the third album. It was the only finished song
we took to Los Angeles to start recording, the rest were all
done in the studio.*

> Son, I'm 30, I only went with your mother 'cause she's
> dirty

*People always pick up on that line, but it was a bit of a throwa-
way line for me. I wasn't even 30 then, I was about 28, but the
line just fitted and sounded great.*

> I said Dad you're shabby
> You run around and groove like a baggy

*That was a reference to my old man, who was a bit of a fuck-
ing Womble. When we were kids he would sometimes go down
to the tip, waiting for people to pull up in their car and dump
stuff, to see if there was anything he could sell. When we were
on tour in the States just before we made* Pills 'n' Thrills and
Bellyaches, *my dad found a jacket in a bloody skip outside a*

nightclub. What was he doing in a skip outside a nightclub anyway? Someone might have died in that jacket but he didn't care. He didn't even wash it, he just put it on and away he went.

You're only here just out of habit
All that's mine you might as well have it

My old bloke was a huge help to us when we were starting the band, driving us around and doing the sound in the early days. But it's hard when you're growing up and growing as people and trying to be in a rock 'n' roll band, and your dad is around all the time. What 20-year-old bloke wants their dad around when you're fully embracing the girls, drugs and the full-on debauchery that comes with being in a band. My dad would end up joining in. When we very first started we used to hide from him when we were having a joint or whatever but after a while we didn't give a fuck and would chop lines out in front of him, or even get the foil out.

So sack all the needy, I can't stand you near me

This didn't mean 'needy' as in the homeless on the street, it means the hangers-on around the band. Like any band who start doing well, there's always a bunch of people around who are after something and just after a free ride.

God's Cop

I can virtually do anything I read
Someone somewhere swam between your knees
Hand me out fish, did some big tease
Oh man did you fuck it, baby brother I took it
Then I pilfered the bag for the Amex gold
Then I pilfered the bag and the Amex gold
Because the lord chief constable knows I'm owed
Oh, and everybody said I told you so

God made it easy
God made it easy on me
God made it easy on me

God made it easy
God made it easy on me
God made it easy on me

'Cause me and the chief got soul to soul
Me and the chief got slowly stoned
Me and the chief get soul to soul
Oh me and all the chiefs get slowly stoned

I like it and I want it and I just don't need to stop it
'Cause me and all the rich got mobile homes, Holmes
Me and all the rich got mobile phones, Bones

God made it easy
God made it easy on me
God made it easy on me

God made it easy
God made it easy on me
God made it easy on me

'Cause me and the chief got soul to soul
Me and the chief got slowly stoned
Me and the chief get soul to soul
Oh me and all the chiefs get slowly stoned

God made it easy
God made it easy on me
God made it easy on me

God lays his E's on
God lays his E's all on me
God lays his E's all on me

'God's Cop' is pretty much about James Anderton, the chief of Manchester Police in the '80s and early '90s, who thought he could do what he liked, and claimed that God was talking to him.

God made it easy
God made it easy on me
God made it easy on me

It's hard to believe now, that the chief of Manchester Police was actually going round telling people that God was talking to him and he believed he was acting on God's orders. It seems mental looking back, that the chief of police could come out with nonsense like that and keep his job, but it somehow seemed to fit in with the madness in Manchester at the time.

Oh man did you fuck it, baby brother I took it
Then I pilfered the bag for the Amex gold

This is a reference to a huge gig we played in Rio de Janeiro at the time. We went to this nightclub afterwards and all these girls and prostitutes ended up back at our hotel and it came right on top in the end, and the police were called. Our kid had gone back with this girl and ended up robbing her, nicking her money, which was why the police were called. She was probably planning on robbing him, but he robbed her.

God lays his E's on
God lays his E's all on me
God lays his E's all on me

This is obviously me flipping the first chorus, so it's now about me.

Loose Fit

Has to be a loose fit, has to be a loose fit
Go on move in it, go on do your bit
Small or big take your pick
Doesn't have to be legit
It's gotta be a loose fit
It's gotta be a loose fit
Don't need no skin types in my wardrobe today
Fold them all up and put them all away
Won't be no misfit in my household today
Pick them all out and send them on their way
Do what you're doing, say what you're saying
Go where you're going, think what you're thinking
Sounds good to me
Don't know what you saw
But you know it's against the law
And you know that you want some more
Oh I've heard it all before
Gonna buy an airforce base
Gonna wipe out your race
Get stoned in a different place
Don't you know I got better taste
Do what you're doing, say what you're saying
Go where you're going, think what you're thinking
It sound good to me
Do what you're doing, spend what you're owing
Pay what you're paying, look where you're going
Say what you're thinking, kill who you're killing
Sing if you're singing, speak if you're speaking
Sounds good to me

Some people took 'Loose Fit' too literally, thinking it was about clothes, but it's not, it's a metaphor for an attitude and a way of life.

> Has to be a loose fit, has to be a loose fit
> Go on move in it, go on do your bit
> Small or big, take your pick
> Doesn't have to be legit
> It's gotta be a loose fit

It's about your approach to life, how you approach everything from your work, or whatever you do to make money, to relationships. For me, particularly back then, it had to be a loose fit.

> Don't need no skin types in my wardrobe today
> Won't be no misfit in my household today
> Pick them all out and send them on their way

That means don't be a bigoted idiot, we don't need no racists in our gang today.

> Gonna buy an airforce base
> Gonna wipe out your race

The Iraq war was just starting at the time, so that was just me picking up on something that was on the news and adding that in. In a way I'm mocking what was going on in the news, but then the Iraq war actually took off just before 'Loose Fit' came out as a single and it actually was banned from the radio because of that lyric.

Dennis and Lois

We all learn to box like the midget club
Where we punch with love and did somebody good
It's good to see ya, to see you nice
If you do it once, well we'll do it twice
We're twice as lively, we're twice as bright
You say it's wrong, but we know it's right
Right, right on, right on
Ride, ride on, ride on

We all learned to wash at the scrubbers club
Where we ring out the dirt with a rub-a-dub-dub
Tell how you think, if you think it was good
Say it loud and clear so it's understood
You take it how you made it, like I know you would
Let it bleed, let it heal, let me sleep, it's no good
So let's ride, ride on, ride on
Let's ride, ride on, ride on

Honey, how's your breathing?
If it stops for good we'll be leaving
And honey how's your daughter?
Did you teach her what is torture?
And if you didn't, well you oughta, do it now

So let's ride, ride on, ride on
Let's ride, ride on, ride on

Honey how's your breathing?
If it stops for good we'll be leaving
And honey how's your daughter?
Did you teach her what is torture?
And if you didn't, well you oughta, do it now

Dennis and Lois are a couple from Brooklyn in New York, who we first met when we went over there on tour in the late '80s. They were this old couple who collected children's toys and were really nice. I remember meeting them and we were quite straight and then later that night when we were a bit twisted, we all thought they were a little bit odd. They became celebrities after we named this song after them, and they turn up whenever a Manchester band is playing New York and know a lot of them, Elbow even used them in one of their videos. But the lyrics to 'Dennis and Lois' aren't about them at all.

We all learn to box like the midget club

This is a reference to the boxing club in the East End where the Krays and all their crew learned to box in the '60s. It was run by an old Jewish guy who was a midget.

Where we punch with love and did somebody good

Sometimes you've got to be cruel to be kind, haven't you? That's my way of saying that.

Honey, how's your breathing?
If it stops for good we'll be leaving

This is another drugs reference. I've been in a lot of situations with drugs around people who have stopped breathing, so you would often check if someone was still breathing if they were particularly out of it.

And honey how's your daughter?
Did you teach her what is torture?
And if you didn't, well you oughta, do it now

This is my way of saying you've got to make sure your kids are streetwise. You've got to make them aware of what's out there, so they can handle themselves. Otherwise they'll end up learning the hard way.

Bob's Yer Uncle

What do you want to hear when we're making love?
What do you want to hear when we're making love?
Can I take you from behind and hold you in my arms?
What do you want to hear when we're making love?
Can I take you from behind and feel you in my heart?
What do we need to relive to bring us close?

Why don't you do it to me?
Why don't you do those things to me?
Why don't you do it to me?
Why don't you do those things to me?

Four fall in a bed, three giving head, one getting wet
Four fall in a bed, three giving head, one getting wet
What do you want to hear when we're making love?
Can I hold you from behind and tell you that it's me?

Why don't you do it to me?
Why don't you do those things to me?
Why don't you do it to me?
Why don't you do those things to me?

The love drug is a bug, that cuts us both up
Why don't you do those things to me?
Why don't you do it of me?
Why don't you do those things to me?

What can I say to you when we're making love?
I could take you from behind and make you live
What do you need me to say when we're making love?
I can take you from behind and then I'll forgive

Why don't you do it to me?
Why don't you do those things to me?
Why don't you do it to me?
Why don't you do those things to me?

*'Bob's Yer Uncle' is clearly just about talking dirty during sex.
I basically decided I wanted to do a coked-up, E'd up dirty sex
song.*

What do you want to hear when we're making love?

*I used to think everyone liked talking dirty during sex, because
everyone I knew or had sex with did. But there's obviously
a lot of people out there that don't. I remember reading this
letter in an agony aunt column once, from a bloke who was
about 40, saying something like, 'I've got this new girlfriend,
and I find it really alarming that she likes to talk dirty during
sex and she says this and that. I'm not sure if I can carry on
this relationship.' I was like, 'Fuck me, doesn't everyone do
that?!'*

Four fall in a bed, three giving head, one getting wet
What do you want to hear when we're making love?
Can I hold you from behind and tell you that it's me?

*I didn't have any problems singing these lyrics when I was in
my twenties and thirties, but now I'm in my fifties it can be a
bit embarrassing singing it live.*

The love drug is a bug, that cuts us both up

*This line is about ecstasy. Because of the effect it had on you,
you'd end up in weird situations. Cocaine ends up in dirty,
filthy sex, but ecstasy could end up in big orgies but done with*

love. But that can mess up relationships when you have to deal with it in the morning. When E first arrived it took some getting use to. I ended up in bed with Bez's missus once, just because this drug made you feel all clean and loved-up.

Tony Wilson actually had 'Bob's Yer Uncle' played at his funeral. I had no idea it was going to be played until it came on. He picked the dirtiest sex song we ever recorded to be played at his funeral. Typical Tony.

Holiday

Hold it there boy is that your bag?
In a small sneak and you've just been had
Is that your scene bin, been what have I seen
Well take a seat, feet, get your feet a seat

You put circle round this this and a circle round that
You put one in the front, and one in the back
Would you show it to your mother, or share it with another
Slow down bitch, oh bitch slow down

I'm so good, I'm so good, I'm so good, man I've been so good
I'm so nice, I'm so nice, I'm so nice, man I'm so nice

Holiday, Holiday

I'm here to harass you, I want your pills and your grass you
You don't look first class you, let me look up your ass you
I smell dope, I smell dope, I smell dope, I'm smelling dope
I smell dope, I smell dope, I smell dope, I'm smelling dope

Holiday

We're so good, we're so good, we're so good, man we've
    never been so good
We're so nice, we're so nice, we're so nice, man we've never
    been so nice

'Holiday' was about all the trouble we had with customs offic-
ers with the band, when we coming in and out of the country
on tour.

Hold it here boy is that your bag?
In a small sneak and you've just been had

It didn't help that I had been done for importation back in the early '80s, when I got caught smuggling some weed back in from Amsterdam, and they even confiscated a porno mag from me, which is also referenced in the lyrics here. I got caught with £250 worth of weed, but then when I later tried to get in to America they thought I had been caught with 250 pounds in weight, not £250 worth, so they thought I was this big time dealer like Mr Nice or something.

You put circle round this this and a circle round that
You put one in the front, and one in the back
Would you show it to your mother, or share it with
    another
Slow down bitch, oh bitch slow down

When I got caught with the weed coming back from Amsterdam when I was about 20, there was this big female customs officer there, who loved the power. She was sat there smoking and took a big fat pen and went through the porno and circled everything in the pictures that she thought was too much, and then she was like, 'Would you show it to your mother?'

I'm here to harass you, I want your pills and your grass
    you
You don't look first class you, let me look up your ass
    you

I've been strip-searched a few times going through customs, and put on the glass toilet, which isn't much fun.

Harmony

I'd like to teach the world to sing, in perfect harmony
Cut it up in little tiny bits, and give it all away for free

Har-mon-y
I, I, I'm on E

What we need is a great big cooking pot
Big enough to cook every wonderful, beautiful, trustworthy,
   lovely idea we've got

*This is another reference to ecstasy and the title is a play on
words. The chorus is simply 'harmony' but I'm also singing
'I'm-on-E'.*

   I'd like to teach the world to sing, in perfect harmony
   Cut it up in little tiny bits, and give it all away for free

*Obviously the first bit is nicked from the Coke song, but the
rest is about ecstasy. It felt so great when it first arrived that
you did want to give it away for free. You just wanted to get
everyone to try it and share this feeling and get everyone on
the same vibe. What other drug has that feeling? With most
other drugs, people are really snide with their stash and the
last thing they want to do is share it. Not ecstasy, you wanted
everyone to be on it.*

   What we need is a great big cooking pot
   Big enough to cook every wonderful, beautiful, trust-
     worthy, lovely idea we've got

That's me just summing up the feeling everyone gets when they first take ecstasy. Sounds naive now, but you really did think it could change the world, if everyone could take E and get on the same vibe you were feeling. The world could be one great melting pot of great ideas and positivity.

Stinkin' Thinkin'

Kiss me for old times' sake
Kiss me for making you wait
Kiss me for old times' sake
Kiss me for making you wait

Kiss me for screwing everything in sight
Kiss me for never getting it right
Kiss me goodnight

I've got to pick out what's in the pocket
So I can leave those pockets clean
I've got to pick out what's in the pocket
So I can leave that pocket clean

An I know that I will always want you
But there's not much that I can do
I'm sweet, will always have to do
Rewind and give me a good clue

And I know just how your mind works
Open your eyes and watch the roadworks
Come on out, it can't get much worse
Sit right down quench your big thirst

I'm tied down with stinkin' thinkin'
Stinkin' thinkin' gets you nowhere
I'm weighed down with stinkin' thinkin'
Stinkin' thinkin' comes from somewhere

Is that what you really want, hey?
Would you like to see me living that way?
The living dead don't get a holiday
Open your eyes, see the real world

Come on down, can't get much worse
Come right down quench your big thirst
Lie around drink your night nurse

I'm weighed down with stinkin' thinkin'
Stinkin' thinkin' gets you nowhere
I'm tied down with stinkin' thinkin'
Stinkin' thinkin' comes from somewhere

Steady job in a small town
Guaranteed to bring me right down
Guaranteed to take me nowhere
Guaranteed to make me lose my hair

I've got to pick out what's in my pocket
I've got to pick that pocket clean

Kiss me for old times' sake
Kiss me for making a big mistake
Kiss me for always being late
Kiss me for making you wait

Kiss me for screwing everything in sight
Kiss me for never getting it right
Kiss me goodnight

Kiss me for old times' sake
Kiss me for making a big mistake

Kiss me for making you wait
Kiss me for screwing everything in sight
Kiss me for not getting it right
Kiss me goodnight

This couldn't be more different to 'Harmony'. Everything had soured and I was in a pretty dark place. We had been to Barbados to record our fourth album Yes Please! *with Tina and Chris from Talking Heads, and it was just a nightmare for me. I ended up famously going off and smoking crack every day because I just wasn't into it.*

I'm tied down with stinkin' thinkin'
Stinkin' thinkin' gets you nowhere
I'm weighed down with stinkin' thinkin'
Stinkin' thinkin' comes from somewhere

When we came back to England I had no lyrics for the album. The first thing I had to do was go in to the Priory, and there was this American psychologist dude there. His whole philosophy to us junkies and alcoholics was, 'Listen, don't be thinking negative thoughts, it's just stinking thinking. Throw all those negative thoughts away, it's stinking thinking.' I thought, 'I'm having that.' So some of the lyrics are a nod to my mood at the time, and what people were trying to tell me in the Priory, but it's also about what was happening around me and the mood around at the time.

Is that what you really want, hey?
Would you like to see me living that way?
The living dead don't get a holiday
Open your eyes, see the real world

The band was falling apart, Factory was falling apart, and different, darker drugs had replaced ecstasy. Manchester had got moodier and everything had got darker.

> Steady job in a small town
> Guaranteed to bring me right down
> Guaranteed to take me nowhere
> Guaranteed to make me lose my hair

Mark Day is a brilliant guitarist but he didn't have much vision. He was happy when we first started playing youth clubs in Bolton and having the band as a part time thing. I always wanted to aim big and he thought I was getting too big for my boots. He also had this thing that had been drummed into him from his dad, that there was no pension in rock 'n' roll. You don't get into rock 'n' roll for a pension mate. I stopped being a postie as soon as I could, but when we did Top of the Pops *for the first time, Mark was still a postie, because you got a pension. So straight after we finished filming* Top of the Pops *he had to get back to Manchester to do his post round the next morning. When the band imploded, he got a job as a door to door salesman, so that 'steady job in a small town' was a bit of a dig at him.*

I also hated the music on Yes Please! *it just didn't sound like the Mondays to me, so that had an effect on my writing as well. I wanted to write the sort of songs that ended up being on the first Black Grape album, but the rest of the band were in a different place. I've always said it . . . the first Black Grape album should really have been the last Happy Mondays album.*

Reverend Black Grape

You know what I mean?

Sell a man your religion
Say I walking down a hit song
A booming business
Buying, selling belief
Standing in the pews
Talking bullshit, bullshit, bullshit, bullshit, bullshit
I want to know, I want to know
Can you feel the spirit of the Lord?

There's nothing more sinister
As ministers in dresses
Gather round some nice black people
While I deliver this message
Kill the message

You do nothing but socialise
And become a menace
Put on your Reeboks man
And go play funky tennis

Can I get a witness?
I said can I get a witness?

Oh come, oh ye faithful
Oh, joyful and triumphant
Gather around
While I blow my own trumpet

Oh Pope, he got the Nazis
To clean up their messes
In exchange for gold and paintings
He gave them new addresses
Clean up your messes

My father's father's father's father
By nature he was bendy
We are the chi-chi tribe
And we are over-friendly

Can I get a witness?
Yeah, I said, come on
Can I get a witness?

Oh come, oh ye faithful
Oh, joyful and triumphant
Gather around me
While I blow my own trumpet
Can I get a witness?

Hey, there bothers and sisters
Hang in there, yeah

Oh come, oh ye faithful
Oh, joyful and triumphant
Gather around
While I blow my own trumpet

Oh come, oh ye faithful
You're so joyful and triumphant
Gather around
While I blow my own trumpet

I want to know, I want to know
I want to know, I want to know

Can you feel, I said, can you feel
Can you feel the spirit of the Lord?

Oh come, oh ye faithful
Oh, joyful and triumphant
Gather around
While I blow my own trumpet

Can you feel the spirit of the Lord?
Can you feel the spirit of the Lord?

I had known Kermit (from Ruthless Rap Assassins) for a few years. We were both smackheads at the time, and the heroin circle in Manchester wasn't that big, so it was inevitable we'd end up in the same back room at one stage. We just got on really well, and I initially brought him in to help a little on Yes Please! *After the Mondays imploded we decided to do our own thing. Everyone had written me off, but I knew we had the beginning of something special. We hooked up with the producer Danny Saber and after the nightmare of* Yes Please! *it was so refreshing to get back to a similar way of writing as* Pills 'n' Thrills and Bellyaches *in the studio. Kermit and I really bounced off each other and it was really refreshing, we just had a great time writing this album.*

There's nothing more sinister
as ministers in dresses
Gather round some nice black people
While I deliver this message
Kill the message

We didn't set out to incorporate a lot of religious references, but I'd come from a strong Catholic background and Kermit had a kind of gospel background, and we'd talk about religion and how ridiculous elements of it were, and that just came through in the lyrics organically.

You do nothing but socialise
And become a menace

That's about Bez. He really did do nothing but socialise, and the rest of the Mondays could never see the benefit of that, but I did. Bez knew everyone, which was brilliant for spreading the word about the band, he was like the internet before the internet. But then he becomes a menace because he turns up at a gig and has 2,000 names to put on this guest list.

Oh Pope, he got the Nazis
To clean up their messes
In exchange for gold and paintings
He gave them new addresses
Clean up your messes

That's just facts as far as I was concerned. I was a bit surprised that people got so upset about that.

In the Name of the Father

It's coming from the side!
And it's coming from the back!
People! Multitudes of people!
Walking up the hills! Go forward!

In the name of the father and the holy ghost
In the name of your father and your holy ghost

Well I don't do what you do, and you don't do what I do, but
    you should do, you
Oh, you've got your voodoo, but you've got no clue
You know no meaty bongo poo-poo for me
Well because I'm no learner, I get away with murder
Going boldly where no man's been before

Here we go, here we go, once again
In the name of the father and the holy ghost
And the holy spirit in me!
In the name of the father and the holy ghost
And the holy spirit in me!
Neil Armstrong, astronaut
He had balls bigger than King Kong!
First big suit on the moon
And he's off to play golf!
Hole-in-one!

Here we go, here we go, once again
In the name of the father and the holy ghost
And the holy spirit in me!
In the name of the father and the holy ghost
And the holy spirit in me!

In the name of the father and the holy ghost
And the holy spirit in me!
In the name of the father and the holy ghost
And the holy spirit in me!
In the name of the father and the holy ghost
And the holy spirit in me!
In the name of the father and the holy ghost
And the holy spirit in me!
In the name of the father and the holy ghost
In the name of the father and the holy ghost
In the name of the father and the holy ghost
In the name of the father and the holy ghost
In the name of the father and the holy ghost
In the name of the father and the holy ghost
In the name of the father and the holy ghost
In the name of the father and the holy ghost

It was so refreshing after being on my own writing lyrics all the way through the Mondays, with the rest of the band not always appreciating my lyrics, to suddenly have Kermit there; this dude I could bounce off, who was absolutely on the same page as me.

Well I don't do what you do, and you don't do what I
    do, but you should do, you

That's just me and Kermit sparring in the studio. We would be throwing lyrics at each other, freestyling, and whatever worked we kept.

You know no meaty pongo poo-poo for me

That line is terrible, it's taking the piss out of vegetarians, which is just another form of belief, but looking back it's not great.

Well, because I'm no learner, I get away with murder
Going boldly where no man's been before

As I've said before, I left school at 14 with no education, but I'm certainly not stupid. I was clever enough to use the fact that people knew I had no education to my advantage, when it suited me.

Neil Armstrong, astronaut
He had balls bigger than King Kong!
First big suit on the moon
And he's off to play golf!

I've always been fascinated with space, and I can remember watching Neil Armstrong landing on the moon in 1968, which was obviously a huge event when you were a kid.

Tramazi Party

Yeah, we're having a tramazi party
Good evening, and welcome to the tramazi party
Just slide inside me and help yourself
We have a wide selection of downers
For your love and enjoyment
So sit down and gouch out at your own leisure

Welcome to tramazi party
Just sit down and slide inside me
We'll get some go-go girls for the party now
If you call around you'll have me
Just like you were Dirty Harry
We'll fill up your carrier bags like a leg of lamb
I've got my boots on the side head
It's full of jellies in the double bed
And no one knows what no one said

Welcome to the nightly
You can have it if you treat it right
Yeah, welcome to the nightly
You can have it if you treat it right

Tramazi! Yer spazzy!
I'm loving the party
Passed round the eggs
And forget everybody

Nobody knows what big nose said
It's full of jellies inside his head
Or something to that effect
Look for the bodies another day

Waheyhey, what did he say?
I don't remember just not now
Oh yeah, I've got my boots on my head
It's full of jellies in the double bed
And no one knows what no one said
Welcome to the party
You can have it if you treat it right
Yeah, welcome to the party
You can have it if you treat it right
Yeah
Trip drip nine, don't do the line,
Watch the unkind
Huffs and puffs
Blood on the cuff
Needle's stuck!
30ml eggs
Time makes no sense
Lick up the dregs
Vapour trails
All in the air
I paid the fare
Well, I've got my boots on the back of my head
It's full of jellies in the double bed
And no one knows what no one said

Welcome to your nightly
You can have it if you treat it right
Yeah, welcome to the party
You can have it if you treat it right

The album title It's Great When You're Straight . . . Yeah *was
definitely ironic. We were on a huge cocktail of drugs throughout the whole Black Grape period. That three years from 1995
to 1998, looking back, just doesn't make sense time-wise, it*

just feels like one long, mad week. When we came out the other side, it was actually three years later and we were like, 'What the fuck happened? Where have we been for the last three years?' Cocaine, heroin, weed, ecstasy . . . we were on everything during that period. But for a certain period of time – it's impossible to work out how long it was in reality, but I'd guess about two years – our absolute favourite drug was temazepam. Forget cocaine, forget heroin, forget ecstasy, the best drug we could all be on at that point was temazepam. It's a wild, mad drug, and you could never remember a thing afterwards, because temazepam did the job it's supposed to do – it's used for psychological problems and soldiers who've got post-traumatic stress disorder from war and things like that, it's not supposed to be mixed with alcohol, cocaine and whatever else by musicians, you know what I mean?

Welcome to tramazi party
Just sit down and slide inside me
We'll get some go-go girls for the party now

Those were crazy times. I can remember waking up in the basement of a restaurant, naked, with two naked waitresses, not having a fucking clue how I got there or what has happened . . . and I had a gun on me. I remember where the gun came from, but there was three bullets missing from the chamber, and I haven't a fucking clue where the bullets ended up.

Passed round the eggs
And forget everybody!

Temazepam would come in eggs and we'd have these parties where you'd just pass them around, and no one would remember anything.

Nobody knows what big nose said
It's full of jellies inside his head

[72]

Nobody knows what big nose said
It's full of jellies inside his head
Or something to that effect
Look for the bodies another day

*We would get a gaff in the woods somewhere and have a party,
and it would all just go west, and nobody knew what anyone else was saying. You would walk round in the morning
and there would be all these bodies just lying around, people
totally fucked.*

Waheyhey, what did he say?
I don't remember just not now

*When you were out of it on temazepam, people would be talk-
ing to you, and you wouldn't have a fucking clue what they
were saying.*

Welcome to the party
You can have it if you treat it right
Yeah, welcome to the party
You can have it if you treat it right

*Temazepam is pretty wild, it could send some people quite
violent, so this is just saying, you need to be aware of how wild
this drug is, and treat it right.*

Trip drip nine, don't do the line,
Watch the unkind
Huffs and puffs
Blood on the cuff
Needle's stuck!

*After a while some people started injecting temazepam, if they
wanted to get a real, instant hit, and this is obviously a reference to someone getting the needle stuck in their arm.*

30ml eggs
Time makes no sense
Lick up the dregs
Vapour trails
All in the air
I paid the fare

Tramazis came in 30ml eggs, and the vapour trails were the hallucinations you used to get.

Kelly's Heroes

Don't talk to me about heroes
Most of these men sink like subs
Jesus was a black man
No, Jesus was Batman
No, no, no, no!
That was Bruce Wayne

Who's got the biggest?
Who's got the biggest?
Whose got the biggest brain?
For he had it bang off
And did a sneak fuck off
He'll surface again

Don't talk to me about heroes
Most of these men sink like subs
Don't talk to me about your big, big heroes
Most of these men sink like subs

Never a sad man
Or a so-called being bad man
Well that's just down to the strain
Well, he hand out fish man
With his centre parting, sun tan
Then cured all the lame

Who's got the biggest?
Who's got the biggest?
Whose got the biggest brain?
Jesus was a black man
No Jesus was Batman

No, fuck, no
That was Bruce Wayne

Don't talk to me about heroes
Most of these men sink like subs
Don't talk to me about your big, big heroes
Most of these men sink like subs

We lead double lives, we deal in sex and beautiful women

Don't talk to me about heroes
Most of these men sink like subs
Don't talk to me about your big, big heroes
Most of these men sink like subs

Kelly's Heroes was a film that both Kermit and I grew up with. The original version of the song was much more hip-hop, but our A&R guy Gary Kurfirst was desperate for a big crossover hit in America, so he made us put a big guitar riff, so it would appeal to white rock kids.

Don't talk to me about heroes
Most of these men sink like subs

Almost everyone gets this line wrong. One guy even came up to me once and said, 'What have you got against Serbs?' I said, 'Nothing mate, I don't think I even know any Serbs.' And he said, 'So why do you keep singing most of these men sink like Serbs?'

Jesus was a black man
No, Jesus was Batman
No, no, no, no!
That was Bruce Wayne

That's just me and Kermit riffing on people from different parts of different religions all arguing over who Jesus was.

For he had it bang off
And did a sneak fuck off
He'll surface again

That could be about someone around the band, someone who had pulled a snide stunt and then disappeared, or it could even be about me – I had it bang off with the Mondays, and then I did a sneak fuck off, and then I surfaced again with Black Grape.

Never a sad man
Or a so-called being bad man
Or that's just down to the strain

This is about someone who is under pressure. He's not usually a sad guy or a bad man, it's just down to the strain or being under pressure.

Well, he hand out fish man
With his centre parting, sun tan
Then cured all the lame

This is a reference to Jesus, or the white Christian vision of Jesus – a man with a centre parting and a sun tan, who would hand out fish and cure all the lame.

Yeah Yeah Brother

You sit at my table, eat and drink like you were my brother,
     brother
I would never, ever in this world would believe you were a
     backstabber
Slash-slashing
You eat in front of my face, and even when my back is
     turned
In despite of your crime, I will pay you no mind
Just leave you to die

Send me a wreath, it's over

You looked in my eyes, they said that you were my soul-
     mate, best friend
When you leave things too long, shit gets long gone,
          and it's too late, late

I told you pure lies, and left you to cry
Open the trunk, for the pineapple chunk
And I'm long gone lady, lady long gone
It's frothy, man

Turn your car
It's over

You were the wise and wonderful, extremely, beautiful chick,
     from out of nowhere
You were the wise and wonderful, extremely, beautiful chick,
     from out of nothing

Won't look in my face, and even when my back is turned
In despite of your crimes, we'll pay you no mind
Just leave you to burn

Send me a wreath, send me two
Send me a wreath, send me that wreath, send me two!

*This is only partially about my actual brother, it's more about
the Mondays and everyone around them. When the Mondays
split, Bez and I were determined to carry on, there was no way
we were going back on the dole. But the others were coming
out with big statements like, 'I don't care if I have to go back
on the dole, I never want to work with Shaun Ryder again.'
Well guess what? They did all end up on the dole.*

*Jealously got hold of the Mondays at the end like a huge
green-eyed monster. The rest of the band thought that me and
Bez were just causing problems. They couldn't see that Bez
and I were just playing the game, and playing up to the image
of what people wanted Shaun Ryder and Bez to be. After the
Mondays split, they had such little respect for me at that stage
that they brought in Everton, who had been our security guard
and was a ticket tout, as their new singer.*

So yeah, that's what 'Yeah Yeah Brother' is about.

Send me a wreath, it's over

*I was finished with our Paul and the rest of the band at that
point. Send me a wreath, you might as well send me two,
because it's over.*

A Big Day in the North

It's your big day in the north
It's your big day in the north, love

Chatte, to share, pineapple
When you smile en coeur le Big Apple
Attention, quelle heure? Georgie Best
La ou mais ou mon ami

Monsieur- achta st-elle noir
St-elle na tu souries
Elle-st ne gros pas
Elle-st comprends

It's your big day in the north, love
It's your big day in the north, love
Grand jour pour la nord, amour
It's your big day in the north, love

Sticks and stones may break your bones
But love, love will always hurt you
Bloodshot eyes scan the skies
Oh my, oh my, oh my

Monsieur- achta st-elle noir
St-elle na tu souries
Elle-st ne gros pas
Elle-st comprends

It's your big day in the north, love
It's your big day in the north, love
Grand jour pour la nord, amour
It's your big day in the north, love

It's your big day in the north, love
It's your big day in the north, love
Grand jour pour la nord, amour
It's your big day in the north, love

Love will always hurt you,

Bloodshot eyes,

It's your big day in the north, love
It's your big day in the north, love
Grand jour pour la nord, amour
It's your big day in the north, love

When Danny Saber first came up with the beat for 'A Big Day in the North' it had a real distinct French vibe, so I decided we should turn it into a northern English take on Serge Gainsbourg. I don't speak French, obviously, but Danny's wife Helen was French, so I just got her to translate little snippets and lines into French, and I just took bits that sounded good.

Attention, quelle heure? Georgie Best

That just means, what time is it? It's Georgie Best time! Most of this song is a bit nonsensical really, but in our drugged up minds at that time, it sounded great.

Shake Well Before Opening

Come and have a go if you think you're hard enough!
Come and have a go if you think you're hard enough!
Rub-a-dub-dub waste the doorman at a club

Come and have a go if you think you're hard enough!
Rub-a-dub-dub waste the doorman at a club

Shake well before opening
Serve it chilled or hot
Shake it well before opening
Serve it chilled or hot

Pleasure, nourishment
A smile of some encouragement
But no, you get it
No you twist

When you're wrapped up too tight and you itch
We're always teasing
Teasing, teasing, teasing . . .
Teasing, teasing, teasing . . .

Rub-a-dub-dub waste the doorman at a club

Shake well before opening
Serve it chilled or hot
Shake it well before opening
Serve it chilled or hot

Nailed your own head to the dartboard
You used a Rolex to roll up your keks

You nailed your own head to the dartboard
You used a Rolex to roll up your keks

You're a rag and bone man
When you're on your own man
We're rag and bone man
We make your own man

Well you eat and you drink
All the chemicals in the world
Won't make you think
Bleak

Shake well before opening
Serve it chilled or hot
Shake it well before opening
Serve it chilled or hot

Rub-a-dub-dub waste the doorman at a club

Shake it well before opening
Serve it chilled or hot
Shake it well before opening
Serve it chilled or hot

Shake it well before opening
Serve it chilled or hot
Shake it well before opening
Serve it chilled or hot

Shake it well before opening
Shake it well before opening
Shake it well before opening
Shake it well before opening
Serve it out or not

Shake well before opening
Serve it chilled or hot
Shake it well before opening
Serve it chilled or hot . . .

This song was born out of the violent times that we were
living in around the time in Manchester. After the halcyon
days of ecstasy arriving, the mood changed and it got a bit
darker, and there were issues with people running the doors
in Manchester.

Come and have a go if you think you're hard enough!
Come and have a go if you think you're hard enough!
Rub-a-dub-dub waste the doorman at a club

That's pretty self-explanatory, isn't it? I had a couple of
incidents with doormen in Manchester who were trying to
make a name for themselves. They didn't tend to last long.

Nailed your own head to the dartboard
You used a Rolex to roll up your keks
You nailed your own head to the dartboard
You used a Rolex to roll up your keks

These idiots were always their own worst enemy in the end.
They would start running a door in Manchester and try to
give it the big I am, but in the end they were just digging
their own grave, or as I put it here, nailing their own head
to the dartboard. Don't come to Manchester and start acting
like that mate, or else you will end up getting what's coming
to you.

You're a rag and bone man
When you're on your own man

Half these guys would give it the big one on the door, but when they were on their own they soon shut up. They were two-bob no-marks really.

Well you eat and you drink
All the chemicals in the world
Won't make you think
Bleak

These idiots were generally full of steroids, and most of them were thick as pig shit.

Submarine

You took the same road
As some sly jeweller
Where you wouldn't get two bob
For everything in the window
Did some bad business
With a spook called Sherlock
Who smoked steroids
And he got me in a headlock
And the boy was so proud
Of the crocodile on his sock
Someone had to tell him
It comes from planet Reebok

Oooo-oooo, honey you're a fool to cry, fool to cry
Oooo-oooo, it's cool to lie, cool to lie

You paid the debt today, oh boy
One thousand parcels in the coal bunker destroyed
You've got annoyed today Sherlock
He did handstands and he back-flipped a lot

He was so proud
Of the crocodile on his sock
Someone had to tell him
It comes from planet Reebok

Oooo, you're a fool to cry, fool to cry
Oooo, it's cool to lie, cool to lie

He was so proud
Of the crocodile on his sock

Someone had to tell him
It comes from planet Reebok

Oooo, honey you're a fool to cry, fool to cry
Oooo, it's cool to lie, cool to lie

(Oooo, you're a fool to cry, fool to cry)
(Oooo, it's cool to lie, cool to lie) . . .

*'Submarine' is just about someone who took the wrong road
in life. We all know someone who's made that mistake.*

> You took the same road
> As some sly jeweller
> Where you wouldn't get two bob
> For everything in the window
> Did some bad business
> With a spook called Sherlock
> Who smoked steroids
> And he got me in a headlock

*It's just about someone who's made the wrong decisions, and
ended up running down a dead end in life, and he can't see a
way out. I knew plenty of people in Manchester and Salford
whose life started slipping out of control. It's easier to spot
when it's happening to someone else's life than your own isn't
it? You might not see them for a year or two, and then you'd
be like, 'Fucking hell mate, what happened?'*

> Oooo, honey you're a fool to cry, fool to cry
> Oooo, it's cool to lie, cool to lie

*The chorus is my take on the Rolling Stones, 'Fool to Cry'.
When Danny Saber was first suggested as the producer of*

the Black Grape album, I'd told him that I wanted to make a record that was a mix of Cypress Hill (who were massive at the time, and mates of Danny's) and the Rolling Stones.

Marbles (Why Do You Say Yes?)

Why you say yes, when you mean no?
Then you say you will, but you won't
And all you gonna do, but you don't
You never do
You say that you know, but you don't know
I can smell your funk through the window
Jesus
And I know that you're busy, and it sucks
And I know you'll swap a kidney for a stone
Well, I saw you swap a kidney for a phone

Well, nanananaaa nana na
Nanananaaa nana na nana na

Why you say yes, when you know you mean no?
Why you say yes, when you know you that you know?
Why do you say yeah, when you you mean no?
I can even smell the smell through the window
For the funk the funk of it
You say you will, but you won't
And if you're gonna get out, then don't
Misleadin' deceivin', goin' to the top
Your misdemeanours just won't stop
Blast off your socks, you sell your kidney for rock

Nanananaaa nana na
Nanananaaa nana na nana na

Why you say yes, when you know you mean no?
Why you say yes when you mean no?
Why you know you that you know?

Snake eyes
Foretold
Step to the gate
'Cause you know you're tellin' lies
Snake eyes
Foretold
Step to the gate
'Cause you know you're tellin' lies
Snake eyes
Foretold
Step to the gate
'Cause you know you're tellin' lies
Why you say yes?
Why you know you mean no?
Why you say yes when you mean no?
Why you know you that you know?
Why you say yes?
Why you know you mean no?
Why you say yes when you mean no?
Why you know you?
Yes
You know

Index of Titles and First Lines

Titles are in italic

BLUE PETER

with

Valerie Singleton
John Noakes
Peter Purves
Lesley Judd

CONTENTS

Do you recognise any of these photographs? They've all been in Blue Peter. Turn to the end for the answers.

1

Hello

Here's our ninth Blue Peter Book, and in it you'll find news of some of the important, exciting and unusual things that have happened during the past year—like burying our box for the year 2,000, and being the very first TV programme to bring back colour pictures of the erupting volcano on Mount Etna. Two of the nicest events have been welcoming two new faces— Lesley and Shep. Shep first came to the studio on 16 September 1971, and you can read all about his training and see how he's grown and developed on page 54.

You might think that after eight Blue Peter Books and fourteen years of programmes, we'd be running short of ideas—but not a bit of it, and that's largely because of *you*. Every day we get hundreds of letters and cards with requests and suggestions for things you'd like to see us try out or demonstrate, and stacks of good ideas for interesting places to take our Blue Peter film cameras.

2

3

4

5

6

7

there!

11

Some of your most urgent letters are about our Blue Peter Appeals. With nine million viewers, you can imagine how varied your suggestions are—so to be absolutely fair, we try and choose the good cause that most people want to support. And also to be fair, we never ask for money, but for rubbish and scrap commodities that can be turned into cash. This way, everybody has an equal chance to help.

In spite of the steep increase in postal charges, and a fire at our Collecting Depot, our Blue Peter Dormitory Appeal was an outstanding success. You can see how your old socks and pillowcases have given 60 destitute boys a new start in life on page 28.

Talking of helping people—up to March 1972, our four Blue Peter Lifeboats had saved 154 lives. But after five years of service, the boats needed replacing, so we gave out an SOS on the programme, and now—thanks to you—there'll be four new boats.

Blue Peter viewers have also contributed lots of ideas to this book. The Tetley family, for instance, let us see their valuable souvenir of one of London's famous Frost Fairs, and Miss Alice Fairhurst lent us a precious possession—a chocolate box—a present given to her father, Trooper Fairhurst, by Queen Victoria. Both these souvenirs have been on Blue Peter, and now they're both in print—so please don't stop writing and sending in your suggestions. In this way, the programme is well and truly *yours*!

Valerie Singleton

John Noakes

Peter Purves   *Lesley Judd.*

Petra   Jason   Shep

8

9

10

12

A STAKE IN THE FUTURE

BLUE PETER BOX

NOT TO BE OPENED BEFORE 2000

"Do you realise there are only twenty-nine years to go for the millenium?" said Peter.

"That's great," retorted John. "We're trying to work out something for tomorrow, and he tells us about something that's going to happen in the year 2000."

The scene was the Blue Peter office on a rainy day in the wettest June for years. The Blue Peter film cameras were rained off yet again, and we were racking our brains to think of something to go into the next day's programme.

"But there's only ever been one millenium before since our calendar began, and that was just before the Norman conquest," persisted Peter.

"Yes, but they didn't have Blue Peter in those days, and I'm more concerned about tomorrow," said John.

"I'll bet there'll be a Blue Peter in the year 2000," said Val.

John looked up from his blank sheet of paper and grinned. "I'll bet you won't be doing it, though. How old will you be then?"

"We don't need to go into that," said Val. "The point is that somebody watching Blue Peter tomorrow is — say, eight. They'll be how old by 2000?"

"Thirty-seven," said Pete, "and they probably will have children of their own watching Blue Peter by that time."

That was how the idea of the Blue Peter tree was born. We decided to plant a tree outside the Television Centre for the year 2000. Under the tree we buried a box for the presenters of Blue Peter to dig up in 29 years' time, and in the box we put souvenirs of the Blue Peter of that day, Monday, June 7th, 1971.

If you keep this book carefully and hand it down to your children, they'll know exactly what is in the box, because this is the first time the contents have been written down. Then in the year 2000 your children will be able to write to Blue Peter, and not only tell them to dig up the box, but tell them what's in it as well. They might even get a Blue Peter badge for an interesting letter!

On the opposite page, there's a plan showing exactly where the box is buried.

The box is lead lined, to be completely waterproof, screwed down at all four corners, and sealed up with an impression of the Blue Peter ship, so that no one can open it up without being discovered.

The tree is a lovely silver birch. It was 6 feet tall when it was planted, and the experts tell us it could be about 30 feet tall by the year 2000.

We wonder who will write the first letter to arrive in the Blue Peter office telling whoever is presenting Blue Peter about the box? You never know, they might invite two old ladies and two very old gentlemen to help them dig it up again. At least, we've given them a very good idea for the programme on June 7th, 2000!

6

We decided to bury a box full of souvenirs of the programme.

We carefully screwed down the lid to protect the contents from the earth,

and dug a deep hole just outside the Television Centre.

The idea was to plant a tree near the box, and in the year 2000, when the tree has fully grown, people can dig up the box and read all about us.

A year later, in June 1972, our tree had already grown four inches.

This is what is in the box

A copy of the 1970 Blue Peter Book (the 1971 book wasn't published until September).

A set of eight Blue Peter Mini Books.

Photo of Val, John and Peter.

Photos of Petra, Jason and poor old Patch, who died two weeks before the box was buried.

A copy of the Radio Times for the week the box was buried.

A piece of film from that day's programme (John's air race from the Isle of Man to Blackpool).

A spool of tape with the Blue Peter signature tune, and Val, John and Peter saying "Hello", Petra barking, and Jason miaowing.

A set of decimal coins, because 1971 was the year they were introduced.

A letter saying who we were, and giving a list of all the things that were in that day's programme.

THE FLYING FUSILIER

We were all so impressed by Fusilier John Read's Balloon Jumping on "It's a Knockout" that we decided to invite him to the Blue Peter studio to show us how he did it. The idea is to clear as many balloons as possible by taking a flying leap from a trampolene. They're not just party balloons either – but enormous meteorological balloons that are used for weather forecasting.

As long as you clear them, you can use any method you like, but John Read, who is a gymnast, had perfected a brilliant technique, using a forward roll which gave him a 20-foot leap.

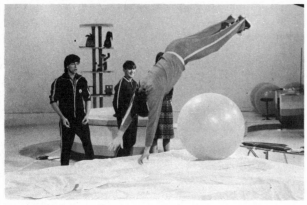

I went first, jumping far too high and only just clearing one balloon.

Johnny, with a little more style, managed two.

But we both met disaster when balloon number three was added.

The champion, John Read, sails magnificently over four balloons.

Mount ETNA

"An item of news has just come in . . ."
BBC Newsreader Robert Dougall scratched his
nose apprehensively and took a piece of paper
from a hand poking into the screen.
"Mount Etna – Europe's most active volcano –
began erupting late last night."

Ever since I was about eight years old, I've been fascinated by volcanoes. All that smoke and fire bursting from the bowels of the earth has made me feel excited and very insignificant at the same time. And now Etna, the old scourge of Sicily, was erupting for the first time since 1960. I was staring at the photograph of the mountain with the smoke

curling from the top, when the phone rang.

"Blue Peter office here. Johnny, we're going to Etna."

"I'll pack a bag and come to the office straight away."

"Better make it Heathrow Airport," said the voice. "The plane leaves in an hour's time. Oh, and don't

I was 80 yards from the hole in the side of the mountain. It was like standing in front of a blast furnace. I could feel my eyebrows beginning to singe.

forget your tin hat – they say there's quite a bit of rock flying around out there.''

Five hours later I was in a DC6 coming in to land at Catania, Sicily. The cabin public address system crackled.

"It's the captain speaking, ladies and gentlemen. Those of you on the port side of the aircraft can see Mount Etna, which is erupting at the present time.''

I looked down and got my first glimpse of the volcano. It was covered in snow, and smoke was swirling out from somewhere near the top. From the aircraft it looked a very peaceful scene – I wondered whether we'd all flown 2,000 miles for nothing.

"No point in going up there tonight,'' said the Director, "but we'll need to make a dawn start tomorrow. Ready to leave at 5.00 a.m.''

Etna is 13,000 feet high. The snow begins at about 10,000 feet, so I was relieved to discover that we didn't have to go the whole way on foot. The cable car was still operating "presso la sommita"–*nearly* all the way to the top. We couldn't quite understand how near "nearly all the way'' was, but we gratefully

humped the equipment aboard and the ascent began.

The snow looked dirty and tatty from the volcanic ash that had blown down the mountain. It reminded me of snow round dustbins when I lived in Halifax and we had a coal fire. When we stopped it was the end of the line.

"Tutti fuori!'' shouted the guard. Everybody out! They'd erected a temporary wooden platform about a mile from the summit – and I soon saw why. The front of the lava stream was only 50 yards away – and still moving down the mountain. It wasn't a beautiful sight by day. At night I later discovered it was the most dramatic firework display in the world. But by day, it was a great grey, creeping horror. There was a sickening inevitability in its sheer slowness. It couldn't have been moving at more than a foot per minute, but nothing in the world would stop it. The flat surface of the stream didn't look hot at all – but I could feel the heat beating back at me like standing in front of a huge brazier.

But this was only the front of the lava stream. It was another two miles to the summit and the crater that was belching out the torrents of molten rock. We picked up the 300 kilos of camera equipment and began the long climb. I've helped hump the gear over difficult terrain before, but for sheer nastiness and discomfort, the climb up Etna will be remembered for years to come. To begin with, we were already 12,000 feet up and the air was getting pretty thin. In no time at all my heart was thumping against my ribs and I was gasping for breath. We had the same problem as the World Cup footballers in Mexico, but instead of draughts of keen, clear mountain air, we were gulping down lungfuls of acrid, burning sulphur fumes. We went up in easy stages – walk a bit –rest – get your breath back – walk a bit farther – and so on, until we were within sight of the summit. Just 50 yards from where we were standing was a great, yawning hole in the side of the mountain – and from it, with unbelievable force, was a shooting fusillade of fire and rocks. It was like the jaws of hell. Gigantic boulders it would have taken a bulldozer to move were being flung hundreds of feet into the air like so much confetti. Here the river of lava was glowing red. Now, it wasn't a brazier, but a blast furnace. I could feel my eyebrows beginning to singe, and yet, strangely enough, my boots were covered in snow.

Molten lava doesn't look liquid or solid. I threw a rock into the middle of the stream to see if it would make a splash, but it just landed on the top of the gone-off grey, crusty blancmange with a crunch, and continued to inch its way down the dark mountain as the stream pushed relentlessly on.

We didn't know at the time, but we were the last people to see the crater for several weeks. The day we left, another great river of lava came roaring down the mountain and across the very path we'd trodden just twenty-four hours before.

It was a strange, exciting, and humbling experience. But we couldn't help feeling just a little proud when we realised that the world's first colour pictures of the 1971 Etna eruption had gone out on Blue Peter.

This was the lowest point of the lava stream. I could feel the heat on my hands and face.

Once the lava has cooled it turns into oddly shaped chunks of grey rock.

Christmas Magic

If you said you were going to transform a newspaper into a Christmas tree, your friends wouldn't believe you! But it can be done. Follow these instructions and you'll end up with an enormous, sparkling decoration.

1 Start by spreading four double sheets of newspaper out flat. Then make a giant set of compasses by tying one end of a piece of string to a pencil and fastening the other at the top corner with a drawing pin. Gradually move the pencil and mark a curve.

2 Cut out along the curve and paste the four shapes exactly on top of one another. You can use wallpaper paste, or mix up your own from flour and water. Leave the shapes until they're dry.

3 When the paste is dry the newspaper shape will be quite stiff. Bend it into a cone to make the Christmas tree shape and fasten the edge with sticky tape. It's easier to make the cone if you snip the pointed tip off first.

4 To make the tree green, you can either paint it or cover it with a sheet of green crepe paper like I have. You'll need a packet of green tissue paper too. To make the leaves cut each sheet into 10-cm. (4") squares.

5 Pinch up the centre of a tissue paper square and twist round several times so that the four points stick up. Put a dab of glue on the twisted bit and stick the leaf on the tree. It's best to start at the top and stick the leaves quite close together so that your tree is well covered.

6 When all the leaves are dry you can wind a string of tinsel round and fasten the ends with sticky tape or a dab of glue. I'm decorating my tree with home-made stars made from gift ribbon. A pin put straight through the star and into the tree will hold it in place. You can use real decorations too — but never use candles or electric lights or your paper tree might catch fire!

7 To make the Christmas tree tub, fill a large flower pot or metal waste-paper basket, or any container you can find with earth or sand. Then push a broom handle or a thick stick firmly into the filling. You can make the container look Christmassy by decorating it with silver cooking foil, and finishing off with a ribbon bow.

8 You can make a tree any size you like just by altering the length of string on the giant compass. Shorten the string and you can make a little tree for the table; lengthen it and stick two double sheets of newspaper together before you make the curve, and you could make a tree as big as yourself!

ICELAND

We've steamed in jungles, frizzled in deserts, sunbathed
in the Caribbean, so last year we thought we'd try something
completely different. For 1971's expedition, we flew to the
frozen North! We picked Iceland as a good place to start—
and from the moment we stepped off the plane, we were
in for a few surprises!

Millions of years ago, dozens of volcanoes erupted and as the molten lava poured out, cooled and settled, Iceland was formed. It's still forming, too! Only a few years ago, the sea began to boil, a gigantic erupting volcano rose up out of the waves, and a brand new off-shore island appeared. It's been named Surtsey, and already plants are beginning to grow on the earth's newest piece of land.

Iceland's a country of immense landscapes. You can look for miles across the rocky lava plains and you'll never see a single tree. In some places it looks just like the surface of the moon, and when we

In Iceland we were taught to Tölt. It's a special way of riding, and we learned to keep it up for hours.

The three little dots are us—dwarfed and deafened by tons of melted glacier crashing to the ground.

Iceland's unique horses were first brought by the Vikings in their Long Ships. Today, their ancestors roam everywhere and are still a vital means of transport.

heard that the American astronauts had come here to train for the moon landings, we reckoned they'd picked exactly the right spot!

But for us, the most extraordinary place we visited was called "Geysir". Here, with a tremendous hiss, hot water spouts shoot boiling water forty feet into the air—straight from the bowels of the earth. We were pretty careful where we put our feet at Geysir, because here, the earth's surface is very thin. Only a foot or two beneath our feet were huge caverns of water. In this spot the hot core of the earth is so near the surface that every now and then the water boils, breaks through the crust and blows off steam—just like a gigantic kettle boiling over! Geysir gave its name to the first modern hot water system, but the 90,000 Icelanders who live in the capital city, Reykjavik, don't need boilers or immersion heaters. They turn on their taps and the hot water gushes out—piped straight from the underground caverns.

Even the water in the swimming pool was different here! On a nice summer's day, the temperature is only about 10 degrees centigrade, but even so, most people go for a daily dip. We thought they were mad, till we tried it ourselves and discovered that the pool was like a nice, hot bath. You don't swim to cool off in Iceland, you dive in for a quick warm up. There are even little pools all round

the edge where you can sit up to your neck in water that's pretty near boiling and come out as red as a lobster!

But not all the water in Iceland boils. As well as the Geysirs, the Icelanders have some of the world's most spectacular waterfalls. We found one at Skoga Foss where a cascade of water fell a sheer 200 feet into the ground and as it splashed up again, the drops of water caught the light and made a brilliant rainbow. It was a breathtaking sight, but even more awe-inspiring were the gigantic Gullfoss falls. Millions of tons of water from melting glaciers thunder over the rocks into an enormous gorge. It was such a shattering spectacle that we were dumb-struck—which didn't matter because the roar of the water is so tremendous, it drowns any conversation!

The first people ever to see the falls were the Vikings who sailed from Scandinavia in their long ships to discover Iceland. We came across some interesting Viking relics – horses! The Vikings brought their horses with them when they sailed, and the descendants of these first horses are the only ones that are used today. They're very small – only the size of a British pony, but for their size, they're immensely strong. They have an odd gait called a Tölt. It's a cross between a trot and a walk, and once we'd learned to ride Viking style, sitting well back with our legs straight and our feet stuck out, we found we could "tölt" for hours without getting tired.

Iceland's beaches were a bit of a shock! The sand's

jet black because it's formed from volcanic lava, but on that black sand we saw a marvellous sight – dozens and dozens of seals! They're timid creatures, so we were as quiet as could be as we crept closer and closer to them. But all of a sudden, they heard us coming – and shot out to sea. All except one straggler. At the water's edge, we found one baby seal who couldn't move as fast as the others because he'd got a damaged flipper. His mother was bobbing anxiously about in the surf, and the baby looked pretty upset, too. We didn't quite know what to do and in the end we decided that damaged flipper or not, he'd be safer with his mother. So we helped him back into the water and were relieved to see her come for him. We worried about that little seal quite a lot, and when we got home, we asked George Cansdale if

we'd done the right thing. It was a relief when George said "Yes". He reckoned that even with a damaged flipper, the baby would have about a fifty-fifty chance of surviving with his mother, and absolutely no chance at all left abandoned on the beach.

It was on the way back from the beach that we came in for a sudden air attack! It was quite frightening. One minute we were driving along a vast empty cliff top, and the next, enormous birds were diving at us out of a clear, blue sky. We jammed the brakes on and stopped – and so did the birds. After a moment or two, we thought we'd risk getting out to see what was up. Wham! On they came again, swooping down on us with their great big wings beating and swerving away, only inches from our heads. We couldn't understand what was happening

We found this lost seal pup lying on the black lava beach.

His flipper was damaged – if we put him back, would he find his mother and survive?

Watch out! A giant Arctic Skua zooms into the attack.

until suddenly, right by our feet, something moved. It was a fluffy, baby bird, so well camouflaged that until it shifted, we hadn't spotted it amongst the stones. Now we knew what to look for we realised that there were stone-coloured chicks everywhere, and up above the attack continued! The birds were Arctic Skuas, who protect their nests by diving and swooping on the gulls, who'd eat their eggs. They attack so ferociously that the gulls are frightened away, and the Skuas were giving us the same treatment!

We drove off very carefully indeed so as not to disturb the chicks, and as we looked back, we could see that in only seconds, the Arctic Skuas had settled down and everything was back to normal.

For us it had been an unforgettable experience – just one more strange happening to add to our memories of that very extraordinary country – Iceland!

ICELANDIC BIRDS

In Iceland, there are many more birds than people! It's a paradise for bird spotters because seventy-six different species breed there. Some of them, like the Pink Footed Goose, fly to Britain in the winter, so watch out for them. And if you happen to be in the North of Scotland, look out too for the Arctic Skuas. They nest on the off-shore islands and along the coast — just as they do in Iceland.

White-tailed Eagle

Arctic Skua

Little Auk

Great Northern Diver

Harlequin

Puffin

Pink Footed Goose

Whimbrel

Snowy Owl

Gadwall

ow Bunting

Red-necked Phalarope

Ian Willis

BLEEP AND BOOSTER

looked fearfully at the silver box he was holding on his knees. "We shall die of starvation!"

"Of course it will work," said Booster firmly. "The scientists said it would – and they said, too, that we were the best people on Miron to prove it! Just think of it. When we get home, we'll be heroes!" At that thought Bleep cheered up at once, and for the hundredth time, read the instructions on the Duolaser: *1 Aim at the object to be doubled. 2 Fire.*

"It's brilliant," he thought. "We've got on board only one stellar pasty, a packet of gamma gum drops, a bottle of asteroidade, and one spare

"Success or failure is in your hands," said the Captain gravely. "An expedition to the planet Tremoritus has never before been attempted – but our new device must be tested, and only you can do it. You have been picked because you are small and your space pod is light. You are inexperienced, but I trust you."

He opened a box which was lying on the control desk, took out a gleaming silver object and handed it over to Bleep and Booster.

"Here it is – the prototype of the first-ever Duolaser. Look after it well and remember your lives depend upon it. When you get to Tremoritus, keep radio contact and report your progress. Do not overstay your mission. One hour's delay could be fatal. Now go, and good luck!"

Silently, Bleep and Booster left Miron space control, climbed into the space pod and took off for Tremoritus and the unknown.

As Bleep and Booster left Miron far behind, they did not speak much. Their minds were too full of the mission ahead and the great responsibility that had been given them. For years, Miron Observatory had reported strange and regular disturbances from the planet Tremoritus. They stopped as suddenly as they started. The whole surface of the planet seemed to change, yet even with their sophisticated scanners, Miron observers could not fathom the cause. They named these sudden eruptions Meltoons, but what actually happened in a Meltoon season no one knew. All that was known was that an exploration to Tremoritus was impossible. The landing surface was unknown, and the distance so great that a Miron space ship would need all her loading bays for fuel. There'd be no room on board for food and supplies, and only just enough fuel to come straight home. But at last, there'd been a break-through – the Duolaser!

Bleep broke the silence.

"Suppose it doesn't work, Booster," he said, as he

fuel cylinder. Yet with the Duolaser we can double them and double them and we'll never run out! And Booster and I don't weigh much, and neither does the space pod. Of course we'll land safely – whatever the surface."

All the same, as the space pod raced towards Tremoritus, Bleep and Booster had their doubts.

Three weeks later, Bleep and Booster were congratulating themselves on the success of their mission! They had landed on the dreaded planet Tremoritus as lightly as a feather, and when they gingerly walked on the surface, they'd found it as solid as concrete. There had been nothing to fear at all and the results they'd got from the Duolaser had been spectacular! The very first thing they'd done had been to aim at their one and only stellar pasty. It had doubled instantly and Bleep had got quite carried away! He'd fired again and again until he was surrounded by the things – each one the spitting image of the original, and every bit as tasty.

It had been a busy three weeks, but now the boys were packing up to leave. They'd had strict instructions to leave before the Meltoon season, and time was running out. They rolled up their sleeping bags, hooked them on to their jet packs and began to load the space pod with the notebooks they had packed with newly gained scientific data and heavy sample boxes jammed full of rock specimens.

"They're going to be amazed when they see rocks like this in Miron," cried Bleep happily, as he picked up a spiky purple chunk and put it carefully away.

"Maybe they'll reveal the secrets of the Meltoon!"

"Maybe," replied Booster, "and they all said there wasn't any life on Tremoritus! What do you think they'll make of my discovery? I'm certainly going to take him back!"

He picked up the little green furred animal with bright orange eyes that he'd found the first night they landed, and tucked him inside the space pod. On the whole, Booster didn't think much of space animals. They tended to be ugly, scaly things, but this little creature was so friendly, Booster had taken a fancy to him and called him Fido. With everything safely on board, they made their final preparations.

It was while Bleep was hard at work with the Duolaser, doubling up fuel cylinders for the return, and Booster was signalling back to Miron that they were about to leave that something happened that was to turn their mission into a nightmare!

Booster had just made contact when he saw Fido jumping down from the space pod and making off across the crater.

"I'm going after him, Bleep," he shouted, "won't be long," and he flung down the headset and ran after the little creature. He didn't hear the faint warning coming from thousands of miles away. "Miron City to Space Pod. The Meltoon is coming. Leave immediately. Repeat. Leave immediately."

Nor did Bleep hear the warning. He was too busy with the Duolaser. When he'd finished refuelling, he gathered up the radio set, put it on board and set off in the direction that Booster had taken. Bleep couldn't see a sign of him, and he was beginning to get worried.

Meanwhile, Booster's chase had taken him far away from the space pod. Fido seemed to think it was some sort of game. Every time Booster made a grab for him, he leapt ahead. The chase had taken them down a steep ravine and into a wide valley like a dried-up river bed. Booster had just stopped for breath when a distant rumble caught his ear. It seemed to come from miles below his feet, and as he looked down, the noise grew deafening. The rock began to tremble and shift, and water seeped up through the cracks. Suddenly, Booster was standing in a cloying quicksand. Way ahead, he could still see Fido skimming the surface, but Booster daren't move. With every step, he was sinking deeper and deeper. He shut his eyes and yelled at the top of his voice – "Bleep! Help!"

Bleep heard the cry with horror and dashed

Dazed with shock, the boys found themselves on the back of an enormous monster, grabbing as tight as they could to its scaly spines as it lurched through the meltoon mud to the far side of the valley. Its tiny head swayed from side to side on its long neck, but its body was so gigantic that it never felt the two terrified boys clinging to its back. Ponderously, its huge webbed feet plodded through the quicksand whilst its long tongue snaked in and out of the cracks as it searched for food. At the far side it shook itself— and Bleep and Booster were flung on to the steep, rocky slope of the ravine. Thankfully they clung together and watched speechlessly as the terrifying monster squelched back into the mud.

"Oh," said Bleep. "How horrible. It was looking for something to eat!"

"Yes," said Booster grimly. "And I know what it was looking for!" For at that moment, he'd spied Fido peeping out from between two rocks. Quickly, he gathered him into his arms.

"And the monster's not going to get us either, Booster. Cheer up! While there's life there's hope!"

"But there isn't," gulped Bleep. "We can't get back to the space pod. It's the other side of the mud— and the ravine's too wide to cross with our jet packs. We'll run out of power!"

Booster didn't answer. Already he'd unrolled his sleeping bag and was laying it out flat.

"Quick, Bleep!" he cried. "Inflate it with your jet pack. I'll tie the end off and we'll use it as a raft!"

"Of course," cried Bleep, "and we'll jet propel it, too! When mine runs out, we'll use yours. We won't need them on the other side!"

In minutes, Bleep, Booster and Fido were safely on board and with their jet packs at the ready, they sped off across the quicksand, keeping a wary eye on

towards it. By now Booster was stuck to his waist and Bleep only had time to grab his hand before he, too, began to sink.

"It's the Meltoon," gasped Bleep. "It's started. Tremoritus is melting. We are the only two to see it, and we shall not live to tell the tale!"

Desperately the boys clung together and waited for the end. Then, as the mud began to reach their heads, Booster let out a yell.

"My foot! It's hit something solid!"

Bleep, too, started to scrabble, and to his delight felt his suction pads lock firmly on. The boys laughed with relief as hope rushed back, but then to their horror they felt themselves being pushed up through the mud with tremendous force – their refuge was alive!

the distant monster. The fuel just held out, and throwing away the empty canisters, they scrambled up the steep ravine, knowing that every painful step was bringing them nearer and nearer to freedom.

But as they flung themselves thankfully over the top, an appalling sight met their eyes. Three more of the dreadful creatures were circling the little space pod! Fido's teeth chattered with fear and Bleep and Booster's weren't much better.

"Now what?" gulped Booster.

"We'll attack," said Bleep bravely, "there's nothing else we can do!"

With great courage, the boys advanced as closely as they dared to the dreadful creatures with their long waving necks.

"Now!" cried Bleep, and immediately Bleep and Booster opened fire. Absolutely nothing happened. The ray guns bothered the monsters no more than a gnat settling on their backs.

"They're not powerful enough," sobbed Booster. "And look what they're doing now!"

The monsters were nudging at the space pod as though it was a football. Any moment they'd tip it over and all hope of escape would be gone for ever.

"I've got it," shouted Bleep. "The Duolaser. We'll make dozens of ray guns and blast them all off at once. That should fix them."

Happily they put their guns down. Bleep aimed and fired. But before their horrified eyes, the ray guns sizzled, cracked and fell into four neat halves.

"What's happened?" cried Bleep, as he desperately tried to piece the useless bits together. "I don't understand!"

"The Duolaser was only a prototype," moaned Booster, "and it's gone wrong. Instead of doubling things, it only halves them. We're finished. We'll never ever see Miron again!"

For a moment, the shock and fear paralysed them. Then, desperately, they began to think. They'd no weapons, no radio, and no jet packs – only a useless Duolaser.

"That's it," cried Bleep. "The Duolaser! It may yet save our lives. Come on, Booster, hang on to Fido and follow me!"

Trustingly, Booster crept after his friend, who was crawling closer and closer to the monsters, the Duolaser poised and ready to fire. One moment the monsters were rocking the space pod backwards and forwards, the next there was a blinding flash.

Bleep fired and fired again. The monsters split into two halves, then quarters – finally there was nothing but a scaly mess – and the space pod was undamaged. Once more, Bleep and Booster had escaped by seconds!

Inside the space pod, they looked down on the terrible planet Tremoritus. Its surface was seething and molten, and everywhere they looked, monsters were rising from the surface.

Bleep shuddered.

"That's the most dreadful place we've ever been, Booster," he said. "When we tell them about the Meltoon and the monsters, I should think they'll give us a medal."

"That would be nice," replied Booster, "but I've got all I want," and he held Fido tightly in his arms and gave him a gamma gum drop for a treat.

FROST FAIR

About once every century, there's a really cold winter, much colder than the ones we have nowadays. But the most spectacular freeze-up of all time happened 300 years ago, in the reign of King Charles II.

Robert Broomfield.

1 The year was 1683, and it was early in the evening of December 4th that the winter's first snow fell on London. In those days London Bridge, with its row of shops and houses, was the most important bridge across the Thames. It was very solidly built, and rested on 19 arches with thick stone pillars.

2 As the weather got colder, ice appeared round the base of these pillars, and each night more and more ice formed, gradually blocking the narrow arches. Within a week the flow of water on the surface had stopped.

3 Crowds began to gather to watch the boats that were trapped in the ice, and the children made slides.

4 An old waggoner appeared with his cart and horse. "This happened when I was a boy!" he cried. "I'll show you how strong the ice is!" and he drove right across the river.

5 The crowds cheered wildly and they rushed on the ice, too. Soon they were all enjoying themselves — even the tradesmen became excited. Christmas was only a fortnight away, and here was the perfect setting for a Holiday Fair!

6 Market people set up a line of stalls, doing a roaring trade in food and warm drinks and souvenir badges. A pieman carried round piping hot pies. Out-of-work boatmen put sleds on their boats and gave rides round the fair. There was a band and puppet shows, and it was even possible to have a shave!

7 A printer set up his press and sold copies of a poem with customers' names at the bottom and the date. It cost sixpence, and the printer made £25 a day!

8 King Charles II himself came in a sledge to see the fun, and buy the poem. He asked if the fair had a name — but it had not. "Then let it be called the Frost Fair!" he declared.

9 At night the Fair became fairyland. Torches and huge bonfires were lit. The ice was so thick that not even this heat could melt it. There was carol singing, hot chestnuts to eat, and whole oxen roasting on the spit. For six weeks Londoners had the time of their lives.

10 Not until February 8th did the weather begin to change. A little rain fell in the afternoon and the air felt distinctly warmer. Then the snow began to melt! No one wanted to find out how long the ice would hold—they packed up their stalls and made for the bank like a huge army in retreat.

11 Next day, a narrow channel of water had opened. Large chunks of ice were floating away. The Frost Fair was over!

Mr. William Bagnall

WHITE-HALL:

Printed upon the ICE, on the River THAMES,
January the 30th, 1739-40.

It could never happen today — London Bridge has wide arches which can never be blocked by ice. But there were other ice carnivals on the Thames, even after 1683, and printers always sold souvenirs. Mrs Tetley of Westcliff-on-Sea actually has one, printed in 1740. She lent it to us to show on the programme and you can see part of it here — a splendid souvenir of an unrepeatable Spectacular on Ice!

Underground at Night

"What do you want to do when you go up to London?" my father asked the night before we left Blackpool.

"Ride on the underground," I answered promptly. This was a long time ago, before I made my first visit to London. I was fascinated by the underground, because we had nothing like it in Blackpool.

Today, twenty years later, it's still one of the greatest underground systems in the world, and something that most people want to see when they visit London for the very first time.

The seemingly endless escalators that will carry you 80 feet below the surface on a single staircase; the strange distinctive smell that you find nowhere else but on an underground station; the eerie silence followed by an expectant breeze and a distant rumble that builds into a rushing wind and a roar as the train bursts out of the tunnel; the dramatic hiss as the doors open automatically to let you on. These sights and sounds have excited generations of visitors to London from all over the world, and for me, after twenty years, the thrill of the underground has never quite worn off.

The London Underground system was the first in the world. It started on the 10th of January 1863 and its route from Bishop's Road, Paddington, to Farringdon Street in the City was $3\frac{3}{4}$ miles long. Today, there are 250 stations and 75 miles of tunnel which includes the world's longest — 17 miles 528 yards from East Finchley to Bank. Two million passengers travel every day on 500 trains, and if you called at every single station on the system, you would travel 250 miles and it would take you at least a day.

Soon after midnight, the last train rumbles its way to the depot, the last

passenger passes through the barrier into the street above, and silence falls along those echoing tunnels.

But not for long. London Transport is proud of its safety record, so every inch of the track is inspected nightly from 12.00 until 5.00 a.m. just before the first trains begin to run again.

One night, I got off the last train at Charing Cross station and joined Patrolman John Gaffley, ready for a night in the tunnels whilst London slept above our heads.

The trains are powered by 600 volts of electricity picked up from two lines running parallel with the lines that take the wheels. If we'd jumped on to the track straightaway, there would have been a blue flash, a puff of smoke, and a blot on London Transport's safety record. There is a set time for switching off the current, but the underground men have a drill just to make sure – you don't take chances where 600 volts are concerned.

John carefully stepped down off the platform and connected a box containing 12 bulbs to the "live" rail. Immediately the bulbs lit up. John climbed back on to the platform, and we stood staring down at the light glowing between the rails. John looked up at the clock, and as the fingers reached 12.50, the lights died in the box.

The power was off, and John leapt fearlessly on to the rails. I felt quite bold balancing along a line that would have blown me through the roof just 30 seconds before. I asked John why there were so many lights in the box.

He said: "If there's only one it could be a dud bulb, but with twelve, you've got a better chance."

When the bulbs connected to the live rail go out, it's safe to walk on the track.

"But suppose there are twelve dud bulbs?" I asked.

John grinned. "Mister – if you're that unlucky, you won't be living much longer anyway."

As we walked along the tunnel, I thought I could hear a distant rumbling that sounded, for all the world, like an underground train thundering along in a nearby tunnel.

"That sounds just like a train," I said.

"It is," replied John.

"But I thought all the current . . . ." I said, looking nervously at the conductor rail.

"It's a battery train," said John. He told me that there were special trains powered by their own batteries which took the maintenance workers out to repair faults on the line.

"Oh, I see," I said, relieved; and then I looked at the 12 foot diameter of the tunnel – just big enough to take a train, with only 3 inches clearance at the narrowest point.

"What happens if a battery train comes down this tunnel?" I asked.

"It won't happen," he grinned, "but if it'll set your mind at rest, I'll show you what to do if one *did* come along."

There's a gap underneath the rails, just big enough for a man to lie under. It's important, John told me, to be facing the oncoming train.

"That way it can't scuff up your clothing and pick you up and throw you under the wheels."

It seemed like sound advice, but I'm glad to say I didn't have to put it to the test.

John was carrying a big hammer over his shoulder, and every so often he'd stop and give one of the keys a clout to bring it back to its proper position. At other places he'd make a note about a piece of work that would have to be done in the near future.

A tiny circle of light at the end of the tunnel grew gradually bigger as we walked along, and at the end, I stepped up on to Waterloo Station. We'd walked a whole 5p. worth along the tunnel.

John went off to telephone his report, and when he came back he said:

"There's a battery going out on a job in about five minutes. You can join the gang if you don't mind a bit of noise and dust."

The battery train groaned into the

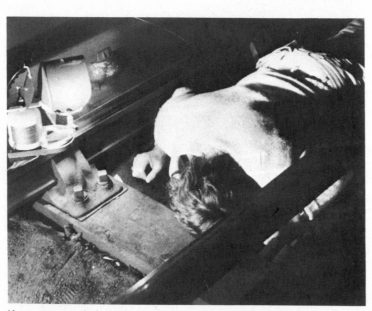

If you get caught in a tunnel, there's just enough room to lie down and let the train pass over you.

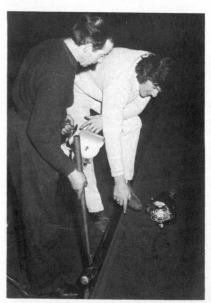

John Gaffley repositioned a key by clouting it with his hammer.

We boarded the battery train with all the equipment and set off to find the job.

We started to drill out the concrete round the old sleepers.

Then we put new sleepers into position.

At 5.00 a.m. we left the tunnel . . . .

station and stopped, but there was no hiss of opening doors this time. In place of the bright red or sleek silver coaches, were open trucks piled high with tools and materials. As we jumped on to the truck, a large Jamaican tossed me a brightly coloured silk scarf.

"Better put this round your head, man. It gets pretty filthy when you're drillin'!"

Our job was to replace some old sleepers, and to do that we had to drill out the concrete that held them in position.

You haven't really experienced noise until you hear five pneumatic drills operating in a long railway tunnel. It was beyond belief!

In four hours flat, we had drilled out 20 old sleepers and put down 20 new ones. The new sleepers were held in position by special jack and brace units until the next night, when the gang would come out again — with a concrete mixer.

But for tonight, that was the end. It was time to get out of the tunnel ready for the first train at 5.49.

The gang leader phoned through to give the all clear, and in the control room the man in charge of the switches filled in a certificate to say that everyone was out of the tunnel.

It was safe to switch on the power.

I was dog tired and feeling dirty as I rode up on the escalator to meet the clear, morning air; but I must admit to a small sense of satisfaction as I heard the distant roar as the 5.49 thundered safely into Waterloo Station.

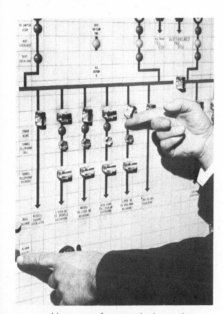

. . . . and it was safe to switch on the power again.

At 5.49 a.m. I watched the first train of the day speeding safely along the newly inspected track.

CASE HISTORY: NGANGA

Age: 6 years old
Found in rags in the streets of Nairobi trying to earn money by showing motorists parking spaces. Has no mother or father.

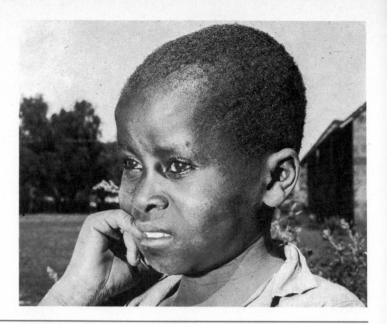

STAREHE S.O.S.

These case histories sound more like nightmares than the truth, but they're only too real. We know that for a fact, and so do millions of Blue Peter viewers–because we filmed some of the destitute boys of Nairobi in our Blue Peter Royal Safari. Above everything else in the film, the thing that stuck in people's minds was the Starehe Boys' Centre–a place of comfort and shelter for hundreds of boys like Nganga, Mwangi and Waweru, who'd run away from their homes to seek their fortunes in Nairobi.

CASE HISTORY: WAWERU

Age: 4½ years old
Found all alone wandering round the city. A policeman brought him to Starehe for shelter. He has no father and his mother is too ill to look after him.

CASE HISTORY: MWANGI

Age: 6 years old
Six brothers and sisters. Mother too poor to afford to rent even one room. Each night Mwangi helps his mother build a shanty hut out of old pieces of cardboard, but because this is against the law, they have to tear it down each morning and build it up each evening. There is no furniture and old sacks are used as bedding.

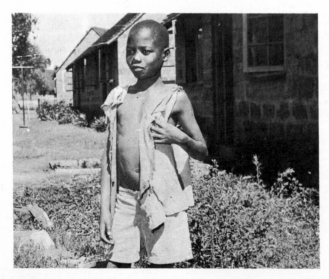

In 1958, a young civil servant, Geoffrey Griffin, was so horrified to see small, barefoot children wandering the city streets in rags that he took six of the waifs into the shelter of two tin huts, and the Starehe Boys' Centre was founded.

During the last fourteen years the Centre has increased to over a thousand strong. The original tin huts are still there, and many modern buildings, too. In spite of this, thousands of boys are having to be turned away. There simply isn't enough room. Last year, over 5,000 boys asked to join, but only 168 could be admitted.

Education in Kenya is not free–so the chances of a poor child receiving any lessons are almost non-existent. Boys run away from home especially to try and join Starehe–so that one day, they'll be qualified to support their younger brothers and sisters. Others just drift into the city–find life desperately hard–and become beggars and petty criminals. Then they, too, hear about Geoffrey Griffin's wonderful centre and beg to be admitted. Apart from getting a first-class education, they know they'll find a comfortable, loving home, with enough to eat and proper beds to sleep in–and that must sound like a dream come true if you've been wandering the streets barefoot and in rags.

When we told Geoffrey Griffin of all the letters we'd had from Blue Peter viewers wanting to help Starehe, he said the main problem was beds.

"We're desperate for dormitories," he said. "It's no use coming to Starehe as a day boy if you haven't got a proper roof over your head and you have to sleep on bare earth, and do your homework with four or five younger brothers and sisters on top of you. Our boys need homes as well as lessons – so until we get more dormitories, we have to turn them away."

A dormitory – complete not only with beds, but shower rooms, washbasins, lavatories and store rooms – was a colossal target. But the Starehe over-crowding was desperate and knowing how much everyone wanted to help, we thought we could do it. On our Blue Peter Appeals we never ask for cash, but for rubbish that can be turned into money. Collecting the rubbish and scrap commodities can take time and imagination – but it means even the poorest person can join in and make a valuable contribution. We discovered that we could build our Blue Peter Dormitory for 20 boys by collecting old wool and cotton – and to beat the problem of rising postal charges, we decided we'd only ask for small parcels. We worked out we would need 3 million of them – each containing one pair of old woollen socks and one torn cotton pillowcase. It was more than we'd ever asked for before, but parcels this size would cost only $2\frac{1}{2}$ new pence to post, which was a tremendous advantage.

We announced our Blue Peter Dormitory Appeal on Thursday, December 2nd, 1971 – three weeks later we'd reached our target! The final Appeal results were even more remarkable – two large dormitories with room for 60 boys. This news was so important, we've made a sort of Blue Peter Dormitory Diary as a souvenir for the millions of Blue Peter viewers who helped.

Geoffrey Griffin, the Director of the Starehe Boys' Centre, knows all the 1153 boys. In the background on the right are the two original tin huts that sheltered six destitute boys when he founded the centre in 1958.

DECEMBER 2nd, 1971: We announce our appeal for 3 million parcels of old socks and pillow cases. This was our contribution!

DECEMBER 6th, 1971: A quarter of a million parcels had reached our depot and we scored them on our giant Sock Totaliser.

DECEMBER 7th, 1971: Down at our Depot - hundreds and thousands of parcels were pouring in to be unpacked and sorted into giant bales of wool and cotton. The parcels were stacked in gigantic piles, higher than double-decker buses. The GPO laid on extra vans to speed up deliveries, and volunteers from a nearby school lent us a hand.

DECEMBER 10th, 1971: Inside the Depot, we were lending a hand too. Mail bags were stacked onto a fork lift truck and unloaded ready for sorting.

The sorters lined up behind conveyor belts

DECEMBER 15th, 1971: After the cotton had been sorted, it was packed into bales and sent away to be processed. The wool was sold to be made into brand new clothes.

The cotton was sent to a laundry to be washed and sold as industrial cleaning rags.

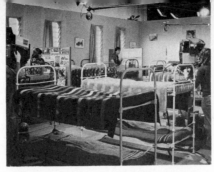

DECEMBER 30th, 1971: We made it!
3 million parcels meant we'd be able to buy our Blue Peter Dormitory. To show what our Dormitory would look like, we built a life-size model in the studio, and Joseph Mutuku - a Starehe pupil - came to the studio to be presented with this plaque.

JANUARY 5th, 1972: Meanwhile, your parcels still came snowballing in - and our Depot was working flat out. Then an unexpected disaster struck in the early hours of the morning. A fire broke out in the sorting area, and six fire engines rushed through the London streets to fight the flames. But thanks to the magnificent efforts of the Brigades of Old Kent Road, Peckham, Lambeth, Southwark, Dockhead and the Divisional Control Unit from Clapham, nearly all our parcels were saved and it was "business as usual" the following day.

FEBRUARY 11th, 1972: Our parcel total reached 5 million, 4 hundred thousand - 2 million, 4 hundred thousand more than our target!
FEBRUARY 14th, 1972: We received a phone call in the Blue Peter studio direct from Geoffrey Griffin in Nairobi saying the extra parcels meant we could build two large dormitories for 60 destitute boys.

The site was going to take another 2½ months to complete.

MARCH 9th, 1972: John made a flying visit to the Starehe Boys' Centre to present the plaque for the second dormitory to Geoffrey Griffin and the boys.

John laid a foundation stone on behalf of all Blue Peter viewers, and Joseph brought 3 visitors to meet him - Mwangi, Nganga and Waweru who, thanks to your old socks and pillow cases, will have a new home at Starehe.

When John left Starehe, the boys gave him a tremendous send-off - and Joseph promised to send us photographs of the Blue Peter Dormitories when they were finished.

FLOWER TUBS

Growing bulbs is easy, and planted in home-made pots they make very special presents. Why not find some old plastic containers and make tubs like mine?

1 Margarine, honey, or peanut butter tubs are just right for little flowers like crocuses or a single hyacinth. I've decorated one by covering it completely with sticky-backed plastic.

The other I've left plain, but I've cut some flowers from a scrap of sticky-backed plastic and used them for a decoration.

When you've decorated the flower tubs, they make good holders for small pot plants, plastic flowers, or best of all, real bulbs that you can plant yourself.

2 Cut the top off a plastic squash bottle and you'll find the bottom part makes a good flower pot. One idea for decoration is to paint it with gloss or emulsion paint. When the paint is dry, decorate your flower pot with pictures cut from old birthday or Christmas cards.

Another idea is to cover the outside completely by glueing on split peas. A coat of clear varnish makes them shine and helps to keep them firmly on the flower tub.

3 This tub is the bottom of a half-gallon plastic can—the kind the washing-up liquid comes in. I've decorated it with string. Start by putting glue round the top of the can and winding the string gently round it. Add more glue and more string bit by bit until the can is completely covered. I've finished mine off by glueing a plait of string right round the top.

HOW TO PLANT BULBS

1 Start by putting some little stones, or pieces of broken flower pot, on the bottom of the tub. This will act as drainage.

2 Damp some special bulb fibre and fill the tub nearly to the top.

3 Press each bulb firmly down on the fibre and then cover them with more fibre, but leave the tip showing.

When you've finished planting, put the bulb tub in a dark, airy place—like the cupboard under the stairs. Don't use the airing cupboard. Bulbs grow best somewhere not too warm. Check every now and then that the fibre is still dampish, but don't water too much or the bulb will rot. Bulbs take about six to ten weeks to come through. When you see that the shoots are well through, bring them out into the light. In only a day or two the shoots will turn green and very soon after that you should have a handsome plant.

QUEEN OF THE SEAS

"Have you heard? She's sinking!"
That was the message that
reached the Blue Peter studio one
Monday afternoon last January,
just as we were rehearsing for the
programme.
Hurriedly, we rang the news room.
"Is it true?" we asked.
"Yes," they said. "She'll be going
down any minute and if you can
get a line, we'll send the pictures
down to your studio."
Quickly the technicians got to
work and fixed up a special
monitor set – and that's how Blue
Peter viewers became the first
people in Europe to see colour
pictures direct from Hong Kong
of the passing of one of the best
and most beautiful ships ever
built – the luxury liner, *Queen
Elizabeth*.

The *Queen Elizabeth's* story is a
strange one. It started in 1936 when
her keel was laid down at the famous
John Brown shipyards on Scotland's
Clydebank. She was going to be the
ultimate in luxury – her state rooms
and dining rooms and saloons were
planned by the finest designers in the
country, and master craftsmen were

engaged to decorate her. She was to be
the pride of the Cunard fleet – the
biggest and best ship on the transatlantic run. Her size was enormous.
Stood on end, she'd have been nearly
three times as tall as St Paul's
Cathedral. Ten million rivets were used
in the building of her 50,000-ton hull
alone, and even the whistles on her
smokestack weighed a ton each!

The date for her launch was fixed
for 27th September, 1938 and King
George VI and Queen Elizabeth were
going to Scotland for the ceremony.

There was tremendous excitement
on Clydeside and reporters who'd
come to cover the great occasion
were staggered when they saw the
new liner for the first time. "Launching
the *Queen Elizabeth* in the Clyde will
be like trying to put a whale in a bath
tub!" they said.

Everything seemed set for a
splendid occasion, but the news from
London spoiled everything. Hitler's
armies were massing; Britain was on
the brink of war and King George
decided that he could not leave
London at such a critical time. So
Queen Elizabeth went alone to
name the ship. What should have
been a great day became a rather

hurried affair, and when the time
came for the new liner's maiden
voyage, all the plans were cancelled,
for now Britain was at war.

But the *Queen Elizabeth* did go to
sea after all. One night, under cover of
darkness, she slipped from her Clydeside moorings and made her first
transatlantic crossing. She turned up
unexpectedly in New York. There was
a terrific welcome, and the passengers
poured on board. They were not the
film stars and rich and famous people
for whom the liner had been built.
They were soldiers, who dumped
their guns and kitbags in the luxury
cabins and crowded the decks in
their thousands as the *Queen
Elizabeth* ferried them back across the
Atlantic to join the war in Europe.

Throughout the Second World
War, the *Queen Elizabeth* served as a
troopship. Hitler was furious. He
ordered his U-boat captains to seek out
the great ship, and he offered a reward
of £80,000 and an Iron Cross to the
U-boat captain who destroyed her.
But nobody won the prize. Always
hunted and often attacked, the *Queen
Elizabeth* survived. Right until the end
of the war, she carried a million British
and American troops to wherever they

"Like a whale in a bath tub" reporters said, as the *Queen Elizabeth* thundered down the slipway and into the Clyde.

The first transatlantic passengers—not film stars and millionaires, but troops on their way to the war in Europe.

were needed most. She was the biggest troopship ever to go to war.

When the war ended and things slowly got back to normal, the *Queen Elizabeth*, too, was restored to her peacetime splendour.

Now, grand and rich people enjoyed the luxury five-day voyage across the Atlantic. We once took Blue Peter cameras on board, and it was the experience of a lifetime. She could carry over 2,000 passengers and to look after them she carried a crew of more than 1,000—and the crew weren't only sailors. There were chefs, stewards, hairdressers, bank managers, shop keepers, kennel maids and even gardeners to see that the passengers had absolutely everything they wanted.

On board, we discovered two cinemas, three swimming pools, shopping arcades, two gyms with all

the latest equipment and vast kitchens where top chefs cooked delicious meals. We'd never seen anything like it. Not only were there about a hundred dishes to choose from at every meal, but if it so happened that you didn't fancy *any* of it—you really would be given absolutely anything you asked for. If you suddenly fancied kippers and custard washed down with cocoa, the chef would make sure you got it—fast!

But all of a sudden, the *Queen Elizabeth* went out of fashion. People didn't want to spend five days crossing by sea when a jet plane could fly them to America in just a few hours. So the great liner was sold to an American company and taken to Florida to be used as a floating hotel. But the idea didn't catch on, and last year she was sold again, this time to a Chinese business man, Mr C. Y. Tung.

Everyone was delighted at his plan to turn her into a sea-going University, especially when they heard she was to be restored again to her original splendour. The refit took place in Hong Kong harbour, and it was just about finished when the terrible accident happened. There was a series of explosions—then a sheet of flame tore through her from stem to stern. The 200 workmen on board dived to safety, but the heat was so intense that the fire fighters couldn't get close enough to save her. She burned for a day and night, then on 10th January 1972, as nine million Blue Peter viewers saw, her great hull lurched over and settled on the sea bed.

It was a sad moment for everybody who loves great ships. The *Queen Elizabeth* was the last of a great age—a Superliner, and nothing like her will ever be built again.

R.M.S. "QUEEN ELIZABETH"

KEY TO NUMBERS

1 Navigating bridge, where the ship is controlled and steered. **2** Hull, made up of steel plates and held together with ten million rivets. **3** Double bottom to hull containing water and oil-fuel tanks. **4** Anchors (three — one each side and one at the bow). Each anchor weighs sixteen tons and is attached to a chain cable nearly 1,000 feet long. **5** Boiler rooms, housing twelve water-tube boilers supplying steam to drive the turbines at a pressure of 425 lbs. per square inch. **6** Engine rooms, housing four sets of geared turbines (one for each propeller) developing a total of 160,000 horse power to drive the ship at a cruising speed of 28½ knots. **7** Propellers (four — two each side), each 18 feet in diameter and weighing 32 tons. **8** Rudder, weighing 140 tons.

9 Stabilisers. These move up and down like fins to counteract the roll of the ship in heavy weather, and are withdrawn into the hull when not in use. **10** Generating station with four turbo-generators supplying electricity to the ship's 30,000 lamps through 4,000 miles of cable. **11** First-class luxury cabin accommodation. **12** First-class restaurant. **13** First-class lounge. **14** First-class saloon and ballroom. **15** First-class smoking room. **16** First-class swimming pool and Turkish baths. **17** First-class

Passengers lounged and sunned themselves all the way across the Atlantic, or bathed in the sun deck swimming pool.

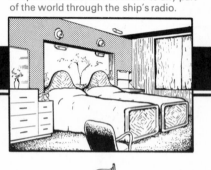

A first-class luxury cabin. From the bedside, telephone calls could be made to any part of the world through the ship's radio.

The first-class sa
famous dance b
cabaret artists e

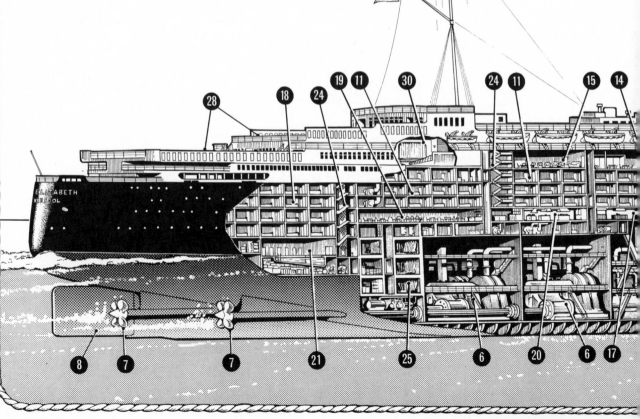

The largest ocean liner ever built – a huge floating luxury hotel so vast that it was possible to walk for 22 miles throughout her thirteen decks without ever retracing a step!

itchens. **18** Cabin-class cabin accommodation. **19** Cabin-class ining saloon. **20** Cabin-class kitchen. **21** Cabin-class swimming ool. **22** Tourist-class cabin accommodation. **23** Tourist-class ining saloon and kitchen. **24** Lifts and staircases between decks. **5** Refrigerated food stores. **26** Crew's quarters and messdecks. **7** Cargo, mail, car and baggage holds. **28** Sun and promenade ecks. **29** Barber's shop, under which is the doctor's consulting oom. **30** Cinema theatre with seating for an audience of 380 assengers. **31** Boat deck with 26 powered lifeboats. **32** Royal Mail pennant, flown to show that the ship is carrying mail – ence she bears the title of Royal Mail Ship (RMS) *Queen lizabeth.*

Compared with other ships......

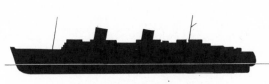

Queen Elizabeth, 1,013 feet long, 83,673 tons.

Queen Elizabeth II, 963 feet long, 65,863 tons.

The new *Cunard Adventurer,* 484 feet long, 14,155 tons.

oom, where nd top-class

A corner of the bridge. The engines were controlled by telegraphs linked to the engine rooms.

ome additional facts:

assengers: First-class 711, Cabin-class 653, Tourist-class 679.
fficers and crew: 1,190.
eals served per day (passengers and crew): 10,000.
tores required for each Atlantic crossing: 100,000 lbs. fresh eat; 35,000 lbs. fish; 82,000 lbs. fresh vegetables; 14,000 lbs. ugar; 60,000 lbs. fresh fruit.

China and glass: 100,000 pieces.
Knives, forks, spoons, etc: 26,000 pieces.
Linen: 210,000 towels, 30,000 sheets, 31,000 pillow cases, 21,000 tablecloths.

VAL AS A PILOT

Are you a good air traveller?

I must admit, I'm terrible. I've flown all over the world on Blue Peter trips, but as soon as an aircraft starts to thunder down the runway, I feel convinced that this is it. The end is in sight. I'm always terribly surprised to find that the aircraft hasn't crashed, and that a few moments later I'm actually alive and being served with coffee by a smiling air hostess.

Have you ever wondered what would happen if the pilot collapsed and couldn't fly the plane any more? In a big airliner it wouldn't matter much because the co-pilot is just as capable as the captain. But what happens in a small aircraft with just you and the pilot, if suddenly he collapses, leaving you, as they say, in the air?

Some people down at the British Light Aviation Centre have been thinking about this very problem, and they decided to run a course for the wives and girl friends of light aircraft pilots. The idea wasn't to turn them into fully qualified aviators, but into people who could get the aircraft back on the ground in cases of emergency.

Having read so far, you'll be amazed to discover that I volunteered to take just such a course. Strangely enough, I don't feel half as scared in little aeroplanes as I do in great big jet liners, but that's another story.

I arrived at Oxford airport and was met by John Curd, who took me straight to a classroom, where, with the help of a model aircraft, I was shown how the various controls worked.

Half an hour later, I was actually airborne in a Piper Cherokee putting into practice the things I'd learnt on the ground. The basic principles of flying are very simple. You have a control column which

Before take-off, Instructor John Curd showed me how to work the controls. The plane was a Piper Cherokee.

you pull back to climb, push forward to descend, and left and right to turn. That's all right when you're up in the sky with lots of air all around you, but actually getting the thing up there, and bringing it back to the ground, is much more involved. It needs a deal of judgement and control. We went through all the basic moves, then John instructed me to head back for base and have a go at landing, with him standing by on the dual controls, just in case I did anything badly wrong.

John talked me down in a calm, reassuring way:

"Bit more throttle–bit more throttle–open her up a bit more please, we're going down a little bit too fast–pull it back, please–pull it farther back."

"Pull back what?" I said as the ground hurtled towards me.

"The stick–pull the stick back," he said, not even raising his voice. "Hold it there–pull."

There was a bump as the wheels hit the ground.

"Oh beautiful–beautiful–lovely!"

I must admit I felt rather pleased with myself but there was no time for preening. We just turned round, taxied back to the beginning of the runway, and within seconds, we were airborne again. This time John taught me some simple navigation–how to use the compass in conjunction with the map to get the correct heading, and how to use the radio to talk to the control tower. Our call sign was XTE which in radio language is X-Ray Tango Echo.

Although I knew that on this flight John was going to pretend to collapse and I was going to land the aircraft on my own, I was quite unprepared for it when it happened.

"What's that village called over there?" I asked. Silence. "John, what was . . .? John?"

I turned and saw him slumped forward over the

When John "collapsed", I knew I was going to have to land the aircraft all on my own.

controls. It's silly, I know, because I realised he was only acting, but I felt my heart pounding in my throat. I wanted to tell him that I'd decided to call the whole thing off, and to stop acting and take me back to the airport at once. But pride wouldn't allow

me, so with a slightly trembling hand, I switched on the radio and said:

"X-ray–Tango–Echo here."

That wasn't quite right, I knew, but a reassuringly professional sounding voice came back:

"X-ray Tango Echo. Oxford approach–go ahead."

I told him who I was and what had happened.

"Tango Echo–can you read the instruments?"

"I think so," I said with no real confidence.

"Tango Echo, will you look at your compass and tell me what your heading is."

If he was going to get me back, he had to know where I was.

"Oxford. Heading 170–over."

Thank heavens I was able to answer the first question. It was like going in for an exam when the punishment for failure was death.

"Roger Tango Echo. Turn left–*left*. Heading 130–over."

I moved the stick gingerly to the left and watched the compass spin round to 130. Then I straightened

Fortunately, Air Traffic Control at Oxford knew exactly where I was, and with their directions, I was guided back to the airfield.

the aircraft up and told ground control what I had done, how fast I was flying, and how high I was from the ground.

"Roger Tango Echo–maintain that heading."

Two minutes later he gave me another course correction, and a minute after that I'd arrived at the moment of truth which is called, sinisterly enough, 'the final approach'.

"Do not let your speed drop below 75 m.p.h.–over."

I could now see the airfield spread out below me, and the narrow strip of ribbon in the middle I realised was the runway. It didn't look wide enough to ride a bicycle along. To my right, I could see a long convoy of dinky cars driving parallel with the runway. I didn't realise it at the time (thank heavens!) but they were the ambulance and the fire brigade. My arrival was being fully prepared for!

The runway was dead ahead of me now and getting closer every second. I've never concentrated so hard in all my life!

The Airport fire engine rushed towards the runway in case I crashed.

A few feet from the ground I closed the throttles.

"Oxford Approach. My height is 500 feet–over." I felt they ought to know.

"Tango Echo. Aim between the two parallel white lines."

"Oxford Approach–Roger."

"Push the nose down a little."

"Roger."

"Tango Echo–you're doing fine–keep it up. Are you lined up with the runway?"

"I'm lined up with the runway."

"Roger–hold it there. Pull the nose back a little."

I was right over the runway now–only a few feet from the ground.

"Close the throttles".

There was the most satisfying crunch I'd ever heard in my life. The wheels had hit the runway.

"Tango Echo–put the brakes on!"

We came to a rather juddery stop, and then–silence. I could hear the birds singing. It was as if nothing out of the ordinary had happened at all. And of course, it hadn't. It was only when John sat up beside me and said "Well done, Val," that it all came back to me. I had been on an ordinary training exercise, not a life and death drama in the skies.

All the same, I *had* landed the plane all by myself, which wasn't bad for someone who's scared stiff as a passenger on a VC10!

Now I could relax–the landing wasn't perfect, but I'd made it!

OPERATION
SURVIVAL

A MATTER OF
LIFE AND DEATH

Unless you live in the country, it's highly unlikely you'll ever have seen a kestrel or a barn owl flying around – and soon, even the chaffinch may well be on the rare birds list.

More and more of Britain's wild life is disappearing. Industrial progress has been a death knell to animals and birds as far afield as Scotland, Wales and Southern England. New towns and cities, roads and industrial sites are eating up the countryside at the alarming rate of a hundred thousand acres each year. Experts estimate that the nightingale could be extinct by 1997 and birds that are now quite common may also vanish as twelve thousand miles of hedge-rows are destroyed yearly.

These are facts that must sadden all nature lovers – for wild-life spotting is one of the joys of a country walk – so I was very excited when Grahame Dangerfield asked me to help with an unusual conservation project – a sort of birds' housing scheme – and it was happening not in a remote spot deep in the heart of the country, but on a golf course only 25 miles from London.

As we lose more of our fields and woods, Britain's golf courses are turning out to be unexpected nature reserves. They're green belt areas that can never be built on, and wild creatures soon realise that golf clubs are not guns, and that the golfers are far too pre-occupied with their games to interfere with them in any way. Grahame proved his point after we'd only been walking on the course for a few minutes. First we spotted some tiny Muntjac deer—a mother and her baby who was only about one day old. The deer had moved on to the course fairly recently, but already the mother seemed to be losing her fear of human beings.

Walking past a bunker, Grahame pointed out some tracks in the sand – they were badger prints, and a few moments later, a hare poked its nose out of a tuft of grass and sprinted over to another bit of cover. Some voles were nesting under a sheet of old corrugated iron – I was beginning to feel the golf course was a miniature Safari Park!

The birds, however, were more of a problem, and that's where Grahame's housing scheme came in. Birds like kestrels and owls will only nest in really old, solid trees. The ones on the golf course were all too young or spindly to provide suitable nesting branches, so the idea was for nesting boxes to be put up. Large ones for the kestrels, with letterbox-shaped entrances–squarish ones with large, round holes for small owls, oblong, branch-like ones with square entrances for tawny owls, and a selection of small boxes with holes no bigger than an old penny for bluetits and coaltits. These small birds would be an important feature of the scheme–they'd help to keep down the caterpillar population which was eating the leaves of the young trees.

We loaded the boxes into Grahame's Land Rover, added a couple of ladders, and set off. The largest trees were on the edge of the golf course, and these were the ones we chose for the kestrel boxes. I fixed a big tawny owl box high in an elm tree, and then hammered a couple of small owl boxes at a suitable distance. We filled the owl boxes with soft saw-dust, otherwise the eggs would have crashed on the bottom and broken. When they build their own nests, the

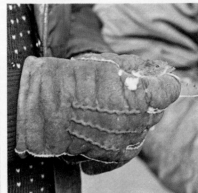

More and more of Britain's wild life is disappearing as new towns and roads eat up the countryside. But all these creatures are safe—the Barn Owl, Muntjac deer and the tiny vole are living on a golf course which is part of an unusual conservation project.

Grahame Dangerfield and I fixed the smaller nesting boxes in the middle of one of the golf course fairways.

All the tit boxes were attached to their own poles.

This large Tawny Owl box was fixed high in an elm tree.

A badger takes an evening stroll safely and undisturbed.

owls don't have this problem, as the holes they choose always have a springy layer of wood shavings.

The tit boxes were attached to their own poles, and these we stuck not on trees, but in the middle of some of the fairways.

Grahame's housing scheme was a great success. When I returned, two months later, nearly all the boxes had been nested in. In all probability, the birds will return the following year, to breed again in peace and quiet, undisturbed by the golfers and safe from industrial development. I spotted a badger taking an evening stroll, and saw more of the dainty Muntjac deer. No one would deny that we need new roads, and housing estates – but maybe golf club

nature reserves are one way of preserving our wild life that is in grave danger of becoming extinct.

P.S. Grahame and other nature lovers are getting support from some M.Ps. Mr Peter Archer has introduced the Endangered Species Protection Bill. The aim is to establish a National Wildlife Authority which would protect threatened areas of the countryside, just as historic buildings are protected by Acts of Parliament. At the same time, M.P. Ray Carter is trying to abolish otter hunting. Both bills could greatly affect the fate of our vanishing wildlife.

LAND OF THE LAPPS

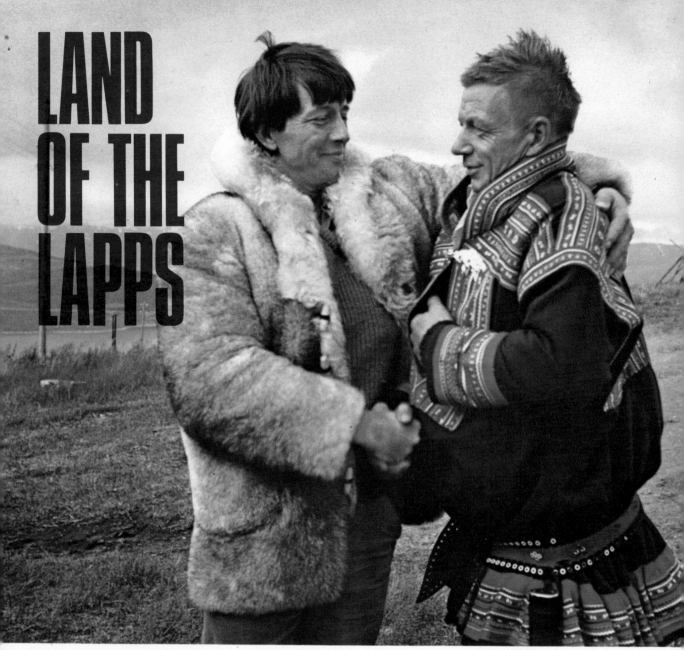

If you want to find the Lapps, it's no good hanging about! At least, that's what Pete and I found out last summer in Norway when we decided to head for the Arctic Circle to see if we could meet some.

The Lapps are a nomadic people — one of the oldest races in the world. They spread right through northern Europe from Russia to North Norway, and in many ways, their lives are still the same as they were in the days when men in this country were living in caves and rubbing two sticks together to make a fire.

We didn't know exactly where to find the Lapps, as they're still nomads. You can see them in one place one day, but there's no guarantee they'll be there the next, because they have to follow their reindeer. When the herds take to the mountains, the Lapps go too.

Once we'd made up our minds to find them, we decided the only way to do it was to make a very early start. It was early, too! At four o'clock in the morning we set out from Trømso. Funnily enough, getting up so early was no problem at all. The sun was shining brightly and the birds were singing, just as they had been all night! That's because when you're as far north as Trømso you're in the land of the midnight sun, and in high summer the sun never sets at all.

We drove through the mountains for about two hours, and in that time we only saw about half a dozen people, so you can imagine it was a bit of a shock to find suddenly that we were at the back of a queue. It was a queue of lorries and cars, all waiting for the fjord steamer to ferry them across a gigantic stretch of water. We were no. 47 in the queue — and we saw the little steamer arrive at the jetty and didn't think we'd a chance of getting on board. But the captain himself supervised the loading. He packed us in like sardines, so tightly that the only way out of the car was through the window.

On the other side of the fjord the mountains were even more gigantic. We drove steadily up them, and there still wasn't a Lapp in sight — or anybody else for that matter. We knew we were getting

44

In the Arctic, we joined the Lapps in a reindeer round-up, "yoiking" after the reindeer who wander miles looking for new grazing grounds. Lapp children dress like their parents in hand-made clothes decorated with richly coloured woven decoration, and inside the Lapp huts, life has hardly changed for a thousand years.

warm — or cold, rather — because even though we were in the height of the summer, there was a good deal of snow around. We were 300 miles above the Arctic Circle!

An hour or so later, we felt like giving up. We hadn't seen a single, solitary soul — when all of a sudden, we heard a peculiar yowling sound! We jumped out of the car and ran through the trees. The noise grew louder and louder, and all at once, in a little clearing, we spotted them — Lapps! There were two men dressed in brightly coloured, home-made clothes, yelling their heads off! The noise they were making is called "Yoiking" and it's a special way the Lapps have of calling up their reindeer. It worked, too, because the reindeer began to gather on the skyline. As soon as they appeared, the Lapps went after them. They were very friendly, and although we couldn't understand their Lapp language and they didn't understand us, they indicated that we could come too. So off we all went, yoiking our way

up the mountainside. We must have walked for miles and miles that day — but the two Lapps never seemed to tire. They're used to it. They'll walk for days on end, following their reindeer as they seek new grazing on the mountainside. Reindeer are vital to the Lapps. They provide them with meat and milk, fur for their clothes, and leather for their marvellous boots. The antler horn can be made into knife handles, and the bones into fish hooks and needles — and the Lapp race would never have survived without them.

When they follow the herd, the men build themselves special mountain huts and we were lucky because we were invited in by our new friends. The walls were covered with fur and skins, and inside it was just like a Red Indian wigwam. There were black furs on the floor to sit on, and white ones to sleep on, and in the middle of the floor was an open fire built on stones with a cooking pot hung over it. We could hardly see, because as soon as we were

inside, our eyes started to water! The hut was full of smoke and the only light came from a little hole in the roof, which was also the chimney.

We were very surprised when we were suddenly given china mugs of instant coffee! It was a sign that the Lapp way of life is changing — but there wasn't a spoon—only a giant-sized hunting knife to stir up the sugar!

Today the Lapps have proper houses too, and cars and washing machines, and the children go to school just like all the other Norwegians. Now they're part of modern Norway, but all summer, when school's over, they live with their fathers in the traditional way that hasn't changed for thousands of years. They learn how to build the mountain huts with their wooden frames and skins—how to catch fish and cook them over an open fire, and how to live like wanderers as the Lapps have always done, when they follow the reindeer over the frozen mountains beyond the Arctic Circle.

The Brontës at Haworth

The West Riding of Yorkshire is very hilly, with towns and villages that cling to the side of steep valleys. One of the most isolated is the village of Haworth, on the edge of the moors, but its name is known throughout the world because once it was the home of a very famous family – the Brontës.

This was one of the places I visited on our Blue Peter Flies North expedition, and as I walked up the cobbled village street, it was easy to imagine it as it must have seemed to the Brontës when *they* first arrived in Haworth 150 years ago.

The horses pulling the covered carts with all the family's furniture had a hard struggle up the steep hill, so the oldest of the six children – they were all under seven years old – walked beside their father, looking eagerly from side to side, at the dark

stone houses – the Black Bull public house, the chemist's shop opposite. But it was the church that their father, Mr Brontë, was looking for – because he was to be the new Vicar of Haworth. Then, as they turned the corner by the church, Mrs Brontë saw the square stone parsonage house that was to be her family's home for the rest of their lives.

The children hurried in to the house to explore. They ran upstairs, and found a tiny slip of a room, which they were sure was too small for the grown-ups to use. Maria, the eldest, said firmly "This shall be our room. We will call it the children's study!" They looked outside at the new garden, and were sure they would be very happy. But their mother was frail and ill, and before she had been long at Haworth she died, leaving the six forlorn little children to look

The Brontë family walked up this very street a hundred and fifty years ago.

Haworth Church where the children's father was the Vicar.

The Parsonage where Charlotte, Emily and Anne wrote their famous books.

after each other.

Their aunt came to take care of the house and see to the cooking and cleaning. Mr Brontë decided that he would teach the only boy–lively, red-haired Branwell–but that the eldest girls should go away to boarding school.

Maria and Elizabeth were eager to learn, but they found the school cold and unfriendly after the quiet warmth of their home at Haworth. When Charlotte and dark, silent Emily joined them, they were shocked to see how unkind the teachers were to their elder sister. The food was dreadful, the school uniform too thin, and many girls became ill, including Maria and Elizabeth. Mr Brontë came immediately and took them home, but he was too late. Soon news came that both the girls had died – Maria was twelve, and Elizabeth was eleven.

Charlotte never forgot, all her life, the moment when she heard this news, and looked around the school where her sisters had been so unhappy.

Now Charlotte was the eldest of the four Brontë children. She and Emily went home, and took up their quiet lives again. Branwell practised drawing and painting, hoping to be a great artist one day. Their aunt taught Charlotte, Emily and Anne to look after the house and cook and sew. Some pieces of their needlework exist to this very day–samples showing a sample of every stitch the girls could do, and their names proudly sewn in, too. But the Brontë

and many famous people in history.

Often they set their stories in the countryside they knew, and the desolate moors, the isolated farms, and the wild weather all became part of their make-believe game.

The stories about the Young Men got longer and more complicated, and soon the children wanted to write them down. So they made tiny books, stitched together, and wrote in them in the smallest possible writing.

They never told anyone about their stories. The books and the soldiers, the moors and the valley, were part of the young Brontës' secret world. It was the happiest time of all their lives.

But they could not stay children for ever – they were growing up.

Branwell, the girls' brother, painted this picture of Charlotte, Emily and Anne.

Anne Brontë's sampler and this miniscule hand-written story book can both be seen at Haworth.

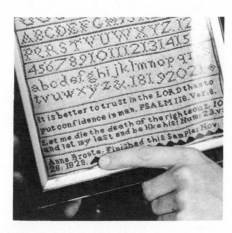

sisters soon got tired of sewing, and their favourite game centred on some toy soldiers.

One day Mr Brontë had gone on a journey to Leeds, and he brought back a box of wooden soldiers as a present for Branwell. But the girls loved them, too. They called them the "Young Men"; they took them everywhere they went, and almost believed they were real people.

Behind the parsonage were the moors. On cold wintry days they were bleak and windy, but in the summer they were bright and exciting. The Brontë children knew every inch of the moors, and here they brought the Young Men, and told each other stories about them, bringing in all the books they had read,

Brilliant, moody Branwell never became a famous artist. For a while he took a job as a clerk on the new railways, then he was dismissed in disgrace. Gentle Anne was sad and lonely as a governess to a family of spoiled children. Charlotte was ambitious – she wanted them to start a school of their own, and she went with Emily to Brussels to train. But Emily nearly died of homesickness, longing for the free slopes of the moors of Haworth, and Charlotte was bitterly unhappy.

Sad, despairing, crushed by the outside world, the Brontës crept back to the refuge of Haworth.

The girls found some comfort. Each evening, as they heard their father's footsteps going up the stairs to bed, stopping as he wound the clock on the landing at exactly nine o'clock, they settled at the table in the sitting-room. They still wrote letters and stories, but now Charlotte persuaded them to send their work to London, to find someone to publish it. They used pretend names, because in those days it was almost unheard of for girls to write books, and they didn't think they would stand a chance with their own names. But they kept their own initials – Charlotte Brontë became Currer Bell, and Emily was Ellis Bell, and Anne was Acton Bell.

After months of anxious waiting, their books were accepted and printed. There are copies of them all now in the room where they were written – *Agnes Grey*, and *The Tenant of Wildfell Hall* which Anne wrote, and Emily's strange, stormy book, *Wuthering Heights*. And *Jane Eyre* by Currer Bell–Charlotte's first book. This was the only one that was popular at first, but it did look as if the Brontë sisters had fame and success within their grasp.

But not Branwell! He went night after night down the dark alley beside the church, and in the Black Bull he drank and talked the evenings away. He knew he had failed as an artist. He made himself ill, and died.

Poor Branwell! Charlotte was heartbroken, not only by his death, but by the ruin he had made of his life. Worse tragedy was to follow.

At Branwell's funeral, Emily fell ill, and within three months, she, too, was dead. Little Anne shared Emily's room during her illness, no one realising the danger of infection, and five dreadful months later, she died, too.

Now Charlotte felt utterly alone. She had no brother to talk to, no sisters to walk with her on the moors, or to read her their stories, or listen to what she had written, round the table at home.

Sadly she wrote down her thoughts at this time. "When I go out on the moors alone, everything reminds me of the times when others were with me, and they seem a wilderness, featureless, solitary and saddening. My sister Emily had a particular love of them, and there is not a knoll of heather, not a branch of fern, not a young bilberry leaf, not a fluttering lark or linnet, but reminds me of her."

But Charlotte took up her work again, though she herself had only a few years to live. Through her, the public came to appreciate better the poetry and novels of Emily and Anne. She wrote two more books herself, called *Shirley*, and *Villette*. She became famous.

And it is because of the books that Charlotte, Emily and Anne wrote, that today millions of people all over the world know about the Brontës, and about the home where they lived together in Haworth.

I explored the whole of the parsonage. The clock Mr Brontë wound each night is at the top of this landing.

Every night, after their father had gone to bed, Charlotte, Emily and Anne settled at this table in the parsonage sitting room where they could write undisturbed.

After her sisters and brother had died, Charlotte felt utterly alone.

PADDINGTON'S GOOD DEED

A story by Michael Bond
Illustrated by "Hargreaves"

Mrs Brown parted the dining-room curtains at number thirty-two Windsor Gardens and peered through the gap at the wintry scene outside.

"I do hope Paddington's wrapped himself up well," she said with a shiver. "It's still snowing a blizzard."

Mr Brown glanced up from his evening paper. "We *have* to go out as well, I suppose?" he asked. "I've been looking forward all day to an evening by the fire."

His remark was greeted by a chorus of protests from the rest of the family.

"I wouldn't like to be in your shoes if you don't go, dad," said Jonathan.

"It isn't the Brownies' fault it's snowing," added Judy. "Besides, it *is* my old pack and Paddington's gone to so much trouble to help. We can't let him down now."

"It's all very well for Paddington," said Mr Brown, making a last-ditch stand. "He's got fur. It's going to be freezing cold in that tin hut of theirs. I know it."

Mr Brown spoke with feeling, for the occasion had to do with a jumble sale in aid of supplying some form of heating for the local Brownie pack, and if the look of the weather through the window was anything to go by he felt he would prefer to add his support after it had been installed rather than before.

Mrs Bird, the Browns' housekeeper, gave a snort as she bustled into the room and caught the tail end of the conversation. "If it wasn't for that bear," she said, "there probably wouldn't be anyone going at all on a night like this. He's been working his paws to the bone this last week. The very least we can do is support him."

And so saying she put on her coat and hat with an air of finality which brooked no argument.

Mr Brown gave a sigh as he stood up and removed his gaze from the roaring fire. He knew when he was beaten and truth to tell, despite his protests, he

wouldn't have dreamed of missing the event.

For the past few days Paddington had never been busier in his life. It all began when he had one of his periodic clear-outs. Paddington usually had one just before Christmas in case he needed some extra space, and on the advice of Mrs Bird he'd taken some of his jumble along to the local Brownies.

Paddington had never been in a Brownie hut before and it had made a deep impression on his mind, for even with fur he'd never felt so cold in his life. If anything it had seemed even colder inside the hut than outside, and when he heard they were about to hold a jumble sale in the hope of providing some form of heating he had decided, without telling the Brownies themselves, to see what he could do to help.

Paddington was a popular bear in the neighbourhood and in no time at all offers of help had come pouring in from all directions. There was scarcely a trader in the nearby Portobello market who hadn't promised to give something and what had started off as a vague idea in the back of his mind had taken on something of the proportions of a miniature "Blue Peter" appeal. Indeed, it had become known in the Brown household as PADDINGTON'S APPEAL, and knowing the enormous success Val, John, Peter and Lesley had with theirs each year he had high hopes of the Brownies reaching their own target.

"Anyway," said Mrs Bird, as they made ready to go, "there's no need to worry about him catching cold. The last time I saw him he looked as if he was all set for an expedition to the North Pole."

In saying that Paddington had been dressed to suit the weather Mrs Bird certainly wasn't exaggerating. Although he was quite keen on snow he also believed in keeping as warm as possible, and he'd taken advantage of the occasion to wear some of his own jumble in order to kill two birds with one stone and save carrying it all in his paws.

49

Apart from his own belongings he wore an extra
pair of Mr Brown's wellingtons over his own,
several pullovers, and at least four scarves into the
bargain. With his old hat pulled down over his ears
and his duffle coat hood pulled down firmly over
that, there was barely room for him to poke his
nose through the gap let alone lift a paw to knock
on the door of the hut, and it was some while before
anyone came.

"How do you do," said Brown Owl as she ushered
him inside. "I don't think I know you. Have you
come to enrol?"

Paddington licked his lips. It was a bit difficult to
hear what was being said beneath all his layers, but
as he caught the word 'roll' his eyes brightened.
"Yes, please!" he exclaimed in a muffled voice.
"Cold weather makes you hungry."

The lady gave him an odd look as she helped him
off with his garments. "What a stroke of luck," she
said. "Sandra's gone down with a rather nasty bug
at the last moment and we're really rather desperate.
Tawny Owl's in a bit of a hole and she's holding
a pow-wow."

"Tawny Owl's down a hole with a bow-wow?"
repeated Paddington, wondering if he'd heard
aright. "I hope she gets out."

A slightly glazed expression came into Brown
Owl's eyes, only to be replaced a moment later by
one of faint distaste as Paddington handed her his
old hat. "You certainly don't believe in taking any
chances," she said. "I hope you don't suffer for
it later."

"Oh, it's not all mine," explained Paddington.
"Most of it's jumble for your sale."

The lady hurriedly placed the hat on a nearby
table along with the rest of the belongings. "How
very kind of you," she said. "You must be what we
in the Brownies call a W.W."

"I'm not a W.W.," announced Paddington,
peeling off his duffle coat. "I'm a bear!"

"A *bear*!" The lady gave a start. "Oh, dear. I'm
afraid that puts a different complexion on things."

"A W.W.," she continued, "is what we call a
Willing Worker."

"Oh, I'm very willing," said Paddington eagerly.
"And I often do odd jobs for Mrs Bird."

"I'm sure you do," said the lady. "But that wasn't
really what I meant. You see we haven't actually
got a bear's section in the Brownies. There hasn't
been much call for it in the past and … " Her voice
trailed away as she caught the look in Paddington's
eyes. Paddington had a particularly hard stare
when he chose to use it; one that could be
particularly disconcerting if you happened to be on
the receiving end.

"Er … I'll just see what Tawny has to say," she
exclaimed, backing away towards some curtains.
"If you like to wait here a moment I'll have a word
with her."

As the lady disappeared from view Paddington
gazed around the room with interest. It had changed
since his last visit. It was now divided into two halves
by the curtains, behind which could be heard a
great deal of chattering. The half he was standing
in was filled with rows of folding chairs and tables
piled high with items of clothing and boxes full of
odds and ends, but before he had time to give it more
than a passing glance the curtains parted again and
another lady in uniform came forward to greet him.

"How do you do," she said, holding out her hand.
"I'm Tawny."

"Are you really?" exclaimed Paddington,
peering at her with interest. "I'm more of a dark
brown myself."

"Brown Owl's been telling me all about you,"
said the lady, giving him an odd look. " I know it's
all very irregular, and I'm not at all sure what Lady
Baden-Powell would say, but as well as the jumble
sale we're putting on a little show tonight and the
Gnomes are rather short."

"They usually are," said Paddington politely,
picturing some in the Browns' next-door garden.
"Mr Curry's are only about six inches high."

Tawny Owl took a deep breath. Brown Owl had
told her that conversation with Paddington might be
a bit difficult, but she hadn't expected it to be quite

so hard. "I mean," she explained, "there should be six of them, but there are only five."

"We're turning the whole thing into a friendly competition," she went on, lowering her voice. "It's badge-taking night tonight. We don't normally encourage it but between you, me and the gatepost the different sections are having a friendly competition with each other to see who gets the most."

Paddington looked round carefully for a gatepost and then when he couldn't see one anywhere turned ... t?" he whispered.

... e lots of
... e for being an
... ollecting things."
... ng," she added.
... ce of bread."
... wards with
... he actually
... bread before.
... unced eagerly.
... o look more and
... as saved the
... y a loud knock

... ring," she
... er full height.
... ests. I'll take you
... s and then I

... irst," she
... hrough the
... Gnomes – are
... t we would like
... ave the right
... in it all to you."
... am. He hadn't
... n, but the news
... play cheered him

... t he even forgot to
... ided him a jelly
... nd himself in the

... of eating
... ake-shift stage
... ctically the entire
... med to be

... n more
... es knew him by
... Brown Owl was
... was gone for
... e returned she

... everything's been
... ed, holding up her
... so many people.
... all come from.

We shall simply have to hold the sale in two parts. I know you must all be dying to get on with the play so I'll just say a few words to the audience and then we'll be ready to go."

With that she parted the curtains and there was a round of applause from the unseen audience on the other side.

Brown Owl turned to Paddington as she gathered the rest of the Gnomes around her. "Now you'll be playing a fly," she said.

"A *fly*?" echoed Paddington, hardly able to believe his ears. "I've never heard of anyone playing a fly before. What do I have to say?"

Brown Owl looked at him uneasily. "It isn't actually a *speaking* part," she said. "I'm afraid you're not really on long enough. Though I daresay you could make a few buzzing noises if you want to and build the part up that way. As a matter of fact you're really supposed to fly out of the window soon after the curtain rises."

Paddington looked at her in disgust. He didn't think much of flies at the best of times, but never in his wildest dreams had he ever pictured actually having to play one.

But if Paddington was finding it hard to take in the turn of events on his side of the curtain the Brown family were finding it equally hard on theirs as they sat listening to Tawny's announcement about the change in the cast.

"Crikey!" exclaimed Jonathan. "Fancy Paddington being in a play. How on earth did he manage that?"

"I shudder to think," said Mrs Bird grimly.

"It's my old section too!" gasped Judy. "The Gnomes!"

The Browns lapsed into astonished silence as Tawny Owl stood to one side and the curtains rose to reveal a woodland glade. Then they joined in the applause as the first of the Brownies ran on to the stage.

Mrs Brown put her hand to her mouth as Paddington followed on behind. "Do you think he's all right?" she whispered.

It was the kind of question that couldn't receive an immediate answer, for Paddington seemed to be behaving in a very strange manner indeed. Clutching his plate of jelly between his teeth, he hurried round the stage several times, making some very odd noises and waving his paws up and down for all the world as if he was about to take off. After a moment or two of this he made his way towards the wall at the back where he appeared to be trying to open a window.

"What on earth's he doing that for?" grumbled Mr Brown. "It's cold enough in here already without making it worse."

"Perhaps he's hot from all the running?" suggested Jonathan.

"He doesn't know how lucky he is," murmured Mr Brown with a shiver. "I'm cold from all the sitting!"

From her position at the side of the stage Brown Owl looked even more unhappy. "I told him to build up the part," she groaned, turning to Tawny. "I didn't say anything about making a meal of it!"

But fortunately for everyone's peace of mind Paddington's enthusiasm wore off after a moment or two, and after circling the stage several more times he drew up a toadstool and sat down in order to watch the rest of the proceedings.

All in all he was getting more and more fed up with his part. Apart from the fact that he had nothing to say, his paws were aching from the effort of flapping them up and down, and as far as he could make out the window at the back of the stage was frozen solid and likely to remain so for some weeks to come.

He sat where he was for a while toying idly with

his jelly when to everyone's surprise he suddenly jumped up again, his eyes growing larger and larger until they nearly fell out of their sockets as he stared towards the back of the audience.

"Gosh!" Judy gave her brother a nudge as she followed the direction of Paddington's gaze. "Look!"

Jonathan's jaw dropped. "Crikey!" he exclaimed. "I don't believe it!"

As, one by one, the Brown family gave voice to their surprise, Paddington hurried towards the front of the stage, his plate of jelly falling unheeded at his feet.

He stared accusingly at a man sitting in the back row. "You're wearing my hat!" he announced.

"What do you mean … *your* hat?" The man shifted uneasily in his seat as all eyes turned towards him. "I've just bought it in the jumble sale. Paid threepence for it, I did!"

Paddington gave the unfortunate man one of his hardest ever stares. "*You bought my hat in the jumble sale?*" he exclaimed hotly. "For *threepence*?"

"Well it's not worth much more," said the man, holding it up for everyone to see. "Look at it! It's full of holes!"

Paddington gazed at his hat as if he could hardly believe his eyes. It had been given to him by his Uncle shortly before he left Darkest Peru for England, and despite its worn and tattered appearance it was one of his most treasured possessions. To have lost it would have been bad enough, but to have it sold almost under his very nose was little short of a disaster.

"Anyway," said the man, "if it's that important it shouldn't 'ave been left on the threepenny table along with all the other things."

He reached down and picked up a large and familiar-looking blue garment. "You'll be telling me next this wasn't for sale either."

A groan went up from the Browns as they recognised Paddington's duffle coat. "Now there'll be trouble!" hissed Jonathan.

In saying there was going to be trouble Jonathan made what proved to be the biggest understatement of the evening.

The words were hardly out of his mouth before it happened with a vengeance. In his anxiety to get to his belongings Paddington tried to climb over the footlights and stepped on to one of the bulbs by mistake. There was a loud bang and with a cry of anguish he leapt into the air and landed on his jelly.

What happened next no one, least of all Paddington, ever really knew for sure. He skidded across the stage, collided with a toadstool, made a grab for the curtains, and as they came away in his paw fell over and went rolling back down the stage again towards the audience.

As he disappeared over the edge the lights went out and Tawny Owl's voice could be heard ringing out clearly above the rest.

"Keep calm, everyone!" she called. "Keep calm!"

But her warning came too late, for by then Paddington had disappeared into a seething mass of curtains, toadstools, chairs, ropes, bits of jelly and pieces of wire, not to mention practically the entire first three rows of the audience.

It was some while before order was restored, and much longer still before the evening finally came to an end.

Although the other items that followed didn't lack for applause it was generally agreed that the Gnomes were the high spot of the show, and with everyone in great good humour the second half of the jumble sale was even more successful than the first; though it was noticeable that having retrieved his duffle coat and hat Paddington took good care to wear them for the rest of his stay.

Being first on the scene at the time of his accident Judy's old section won the lion's share of the proficiency badges. There were several for first aid, two needlework badges for repairing the curtains in record time, and quite a number for being animal lovers. As Tawny Owl put it during her closing speech, they were really only meant to be given to those who took care of a pet for three months, but one evening with Paddington was more than sufficient.

Paddington looked most offended at this last remark, but he brightened considerably as he

listened to the rest of the speech.

"I've been hearing all about this young bear's efforts on our behalf," said Tawny Owl, as she presented Paddington with a special 'Collectors' badge of his own, "and I must say we're very lucky in our friends. We've not only made enough money out of our jumble sale to pay for the heating to be put in but we've enough left over to run it for several winters to come."

"I really think," she concluded, amid general applause, "we ought to thank both Paddington and our lucky stars for a most successful evening!"

As the Browns made their way home shortly afterwards Judy took hold of Paddington's paw. "I wonder what they're called?" she said. "Your lucky stars, I mean. It would be nice to know their names."

Paddington paused for a moment and peered thoughtfully up at the sky. "I think," he said at last, "they're probably called Val, John, Peter and Lesley. After all, if I hadn't seen all their 'Blue Peter' appeals I don't suppose I would ever have thought of running one myself!"

SHEP

OUR BLUE PETER PUPPY

8 weeks old—Shep's first photograph.

7 months old—with his Border Collie features developing.

One thing every pet owner has to face is the sad fact that sooner or later his pet will die. Knowing this doesn't make losing a pet any easier—but at least you can console yourself with the thought that you looked after your budgie or your kitten or your goldfish as well as you possibly could.

This is how I cheered myself up after Patch died, but although people were very kind, and offers of new puppies reached the Blue Peter office by every post, at that time I still missed Patch far too much to want to fill his place. As well as that, I knew that during the summer I'd be away on our "Blue Peter Flies North" expedition, which would make it impossible to start to train a new puppy right away. But strangely enough, it was while we were in Iceland that I realised exactly the kind of dog I wanted for our new Blue Peter puppy. I was thinking about some of the interesting people who'd visited the Blue Peter studio during the past year, and two men stuck in my mind. They'd brought their dogs to demonstrate some of the rigorous obedience tests held at Crufts—the world's top Dog Show. Both the dogs were superb—they were alert, obedient and very, very intelligent, and they were both Border Collies. In a flash my mind was made up—and seven weeks later, a new member of the team made his first appearance on Blue Peter—a black, white and tan Border Collie puppy!

Our puppy was quite a challenge. First of all he had to have a suitable name, and although he was unlikely to end up as a working dog—rounding up sheep for a living—by tradition, all Border Collies should have short, simple names—ones that would be easy for shepherds calling them over the fells and fields.

We looked at some old Sheep Dog Trials programmes—and sure enough, all the names were short like Fly, Gyp, Rex, Moss, Tarn, Flash, Spot, Rod, Nell and Ben. We asked *you* watching at home to send in *your* ideas, and said we'd choose the most popular suggestion. That's how Shep got his name—and I'll always remember him sitting on top of a pile of

A family portrait—Shep's mother, Sadghyl Fell, on the left, and his father, Plas Major Craig of Sadghyl, on the right.

54

At 6 months Shep would sit in front of me on command.

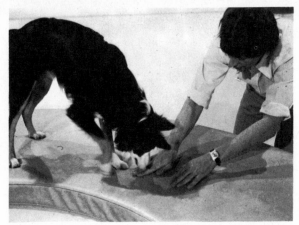
Playing with my hands was an important part of Shep's training.

thousands of postcards in the studio, quietly chewing his way through them whilst our backs were turned !

But the main reason why Shep's been a challenge is that Border Collies need slightly different training from most other dogs. Quite frankly, after bringing up Patch and Petra and puppy walking Cindy and Honey, our two Blue Peter Guide Dogs for the blind, we thought we knew everything about training puppies – but we were wrong.

Working Border Collies respond to hand, voice or whistle "commands", often at a very great distance away from the shepherd or farmer. They have a particularly keen reaction to the sight of something moving, and to sounds as well, and they're a much more sensitive type of dog than most family pets. This meant that I had to try and anticipate Shep's reactions to movements, learn not to shout at him or be at all rough with him, and I also had to make him really interested in me ! Very often I have to make use of "Distant Control" like the Crufts Obedience competitors – for this you MUST have a dog who has acquired the *habit* of paying attention to you willingly.

Bringing up a puppy to work happily in a TV studio also needs a bit of extra care. When he was very small, Shep had to be carefully introduced to all the noisy or peculiar things we had on the programme so that he didn't become apprehensive. But we seem to have been successful, as Shep loves his days in the studio.

Teaching Shep to play with my hands was enormously important. It taught him to *concentrate* on me, and it's something that he had to learn whilst he was a puppy – you can't easily teach it to an older dog. This hand watching was very important later in Shep's development, whatever I was teaching him to do. I started off by sitting on the floor, and tapping and waggling my hands. Shep was attracted by the sight and noise and began to play with my hands. He was concentrating like mad, and this was good – even though he had very sharp teeth ! In the end, I'm glad to say he learned not to bite too hard.

You may be thinking that all this seems like playing, not training. But it is by playing with Shep that I gain his concentration and interest. Border Collies in training need lots of attention from the person they

are to work with. I played another game with Shep that encouraged his attention and built up his confidence in me. Sometimes, when he jumped up, I'd push him off in a very friendly way, saying something like "Get off with you !" He'd bounce back, eager for more, and each time I'd push him off. It was fairly rumbustious, and I had to make sure there was no furniture in the way – but I'd keep it up until Shep was exhausted and then end up making a big fuss of him.

I taught Shep to use his nose by encouraging him to hunt for his favourite titbit. I started him off by giving him a bit of biscuit, and then hiding another bit in my pocket. In the early days I'd always let him see where I was "hiding" the biscuits – and after he'd got used to sniffing round my pockets and up my sleeves, I'd hide them under tables and carpets and send him off, asking him to "find it".

This training was done like a game – I was never cross if he *didn't* find the biscuit – if he was baffled, I'd just show him where it was, praising him all the time. All dogs react to praise – sensitive dogs like Border Collies even more so than others.

All these exercises were teaching Shep that I was

Shep used this puppy pen until he learned to come when he was called.

Grooming became increasingly important as Shep's hair grew longer.

At 8 months Shep could sit on the scales by himself.

Shep grew fast—18·5 cms. in 5 months.

interesting and worth watching, and soon his eyes were following my every move — even if there were quite a lot of intriguing distractions near by.

Coming when he was called was another of Shep's first lessons. I always stroked and praised him when he arrived — no matter how long he took to come to me, or what he'd been doing. I tried to sound happy and pleasant when I called him — after all, no one will come willingly to someone much bigger, if the bigger person sounds very cross and bad-tempered. The crosser the master sounds, the more reluctant the pup will be to come to him. Another tip I learned was never to walk towards or go and collect Shep after I'd called him. I'd always walk *away* from him, and it worked — but you must start this *very* early on, not when the pup's beginning to grow up.

So by the time Shep was six months old, he could do the following things:

Come when he was called;
Go to bed when he was told;
Sit in front of me on command;

Understand a release command;
Know what I meant when I said "no";
Play with my hands;
Was learning to use his nose.

Of course, as well as training him, I was grooming him every day — very important as his hair became longer and stragglier — weighing and measuring him to check on his development, and generally seeing he was well looked after and cared for. I took him for daily walks to introduce him to new sights, sounds and smells — to say nothing of other animals. I'll never forget his reaction when he met his first litter of piglets!

Now he's older, Shep's doing more advanced training. He'll never be a working sheep dog, but all the same, we're trying to see that all his Border Collie instincts are used to their best advantage. His training's so interesting, I think I'm enjoying it as much as he is — and watching a Border Collie puppy grow up has been one of my very best Blue Peter assignments!

I took Shep for daily walks to introduce him to new sights and sounds and smells. We always ended up with a game with Shep off the lead.

SPUD-WICHES

Here's a tasty snack for tea or supper. Spud-wiches are best eaten hot. The ingredients are all very simple—ones you're likely to have handy without doing any special shopping.

Next time you invite your friends to tea, why not try them out?

1 You will need:
1 lb. of mashed, cooked potato, 2 eggs, corned beef, or any other tinned meat, milk, tomato sauce, a teaspoon of salt and pepper.

2 Mash the potatoes finely until they are dry and flaky (a good tip is to drain the water from them after they're cooked, and return the saucepan to the stove for a few seconds, letting them "cook" without water. This will evaporate excess moisture).

3 Divide the mixture in two and flatten one half to about $\frac{1}{4}$" thick (6 mm.) Spread with tomato sauce (or horse-radish, mustard, or any favourite flavour), cover with slices of meat, about the same thickness, then more sauce and a final layer of the other half of the potato.

4 Beat the egg yolks with a little milk and pour into a shallow dish. Cut the potato sandwiches to a convenient size, dip each one into a saucer of seasoned flour, then the egg yolk and milk mixture, and finally the flour again.

5 Fry the spud-wiches in hot, shallow fat, turning them so that they brown on all sides. If you are not allowed to use a frying pan, ask a grown up to help with this stage. Serve hot with gravy, or a sauce made from tinned soup.

"BREAK YOUR LEG – BREAK YOUR NECK!"

Imagine saying that to someone about to perform an astonishing feat–where a single falter could send him hurtling to his death. But that's what we wished the incredible Karl Wallenda when he came to the BBC's Television Centre and walked along a wire stretched outside our studio 50 feet long and 60 feet off the ground.

"Don't wish me good luck," implored Karl. "For high wire walkers that means *bad* luck. Say 'Hals und Beinbruch!'"
We struggled with the German and gave up.
"What does it mean?" we asked. Karl smiled–
"Break your leg–break your neck!"

Karl Wallenda is, without doubt, the most famous high wire walker in the world. Two years ago, millions of people in Britain sat eyes glued to their TV sets as they watched 65-year-old Karl walk one thousand one hundred feet along a wire seven hundred and forty feet high across the Tallulah Gorge in Georgia, U.S.A.

Not content with this death defying feat of balance, when he was half way across, Mr Wallenda actually stood on his head, saying quite calmly into the small microphone fixed around his neck that he was doing it for the BBC viewers in Britain!

As soon as we heard that Karl Wallenda was to visit Britain for the first time since he left for America 33 years ago, we hoped against hope we'd persuade him to do a high wire walk specially for us. To actually talk to the world's expert, and see him in action, would be the chance of a lifetime.

One day, a cable arrived from Florida :–

```
DELIGHTED TO APPEAR ON BLUE PETER IF
SUITABLE RIGGING AVAILABLE.

        KARL WALLENDA
```

The rigging was a tremendous problem. With a man's life at stake you can take no chances. Karl said he would walk along a wire stretching from the BBC Canteen block right over to the main TV Centre building, and this involved finding the right wire ($\frac{5}{8}$ of an inch thick), fixing it to specially constructed scaffolding, which in turn had to be equally secure, and also finding a lightweight steel pole, 22 feet long, for Karl to balance with as he walked.

We thought the morning of the walk would be tense. It was for *us*, but not for Karl. He inspected the equipment, tested his pole, said he was delighted with everything, and then, just as though he was going to catch a train and had a little time to wait on the platform–sat down on the roof for a bit of a chat!

Anyone as amazing as Karl is bound to have an interesting story to tell. At least four generations of Wallendas have worked in the circus, and Karl made *his* first appearance in the ring when he was just five years old, performing his first public wire walk when he was aged fifteen.

High wire walking truly is dicing with death–and it was in America that Karl had his worst accident. In 1962, the seven Wallendas were forming

High up on the roof of the Television Centre, Karl sat and chatted with us before his Blue Peter walk. Like most old circus families, Karl's is a mixture of nationalities. One grandfather was English, the other had a circus in Liège in Belgium, and other ancestors include Germans and Czechs.

With a lightweight steel pole to help him balance, Karl walked 50 feet along a wire only $\frac{5}{8}$ of an inch thick. There was an anxious moment as one end of the pole brushed only a few centimetres from the canteen wall—conditions were certainly not ideal. High wire walkers need plenty of space.

a human pyramid, 40 feet above the circus ring. The base of the pyramid was four men on bicycles—all on a narrow wire, $\frac{5}{8}$ of an inch thick! One of the team made a false move, the whole pyramid collapsed, and while Karl miraculously survived, his nephew and son-in-law were killed, and his own son was paralysed for life.

But Karl Wallenda didn't give up. Eight years later he was making his staggering Tallulah Gorge walk—and two years after that, here he was with us ready to perform at the TV Centre.

Karl wore no special costume for our walk—except for his shoes. They looked rather like ballet shoes, but with no straps and with exceedingly thin leather soles. He also refused any kind of safety net—he hasn't worked with one for 44 years.

When Karl took up his pole and stepped on to the wire, our hearts were in our mouths—one false move and he would have crashed 60 feet to the ground. As he approached the middle of the wire he stopped—

"Shall I stand on my head?" he asked.

It was unbearable! Very slowly Karl edged his body forward—bent over—curled up and stretched his legs high into the air. He wobbled and stood up.

"Not very good," said Karl. "I will do it again."

"You don't have to!" I stammered, but it was too late. Sixty-seven year-old Karl stood on his head *again*—and thank goodness, this time he was satisfied!

Apart from his unusual shoes with their paper-thin leather soles, Karl wore no special costume for his high wire walk.

For the most outstanding feat ever performed on our programme, we gave Karl our highest award—a gold Blue Peter badge. And we were very proud indeed when he said he'd wear it as a mascot on his next high wire walk. Wherever and whenever that is, we'll all be crossing our fingers and wishing Karl—

"Break your leg—break your neck!"

  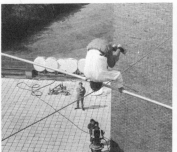 

Not content with his perilous feat of walking along the narrow wire, when he was half way across, Karl decided he'd stand on his head. One false move would have sent him crashing 60 feet to the ground below! Quite frankly, we couldn't wait for the walk to end. Sweat was pouring off us as Karl reached the platform on the TV Centre roof. But Karl himself was quite unruffled—he'd have done it again for two pins.

PREHISTORIC PETS

If you said you'd got a prehistoric monster at the bottom of your garden, no one would believe you. But if you've got a tortoise as a pet, you've got the nearest thing to it! It's an odd thought, but modern tortoises are the direct descendants of creatures that walked the earth long before there were any people, and no doubt, Freda's ancestors, who lived in the primeval swamps, had many a nasty shock when the Dinosaurs thundered by!

Although the Giant Lizards have long since disappeared, the tortoise must have been built for survival. And very good pets they make, too. They're easy to look after and cheap to feed, and although they're reptiles, they don't give people the shudders in the same way that snakes and lizards do. Our Freda, certainly, is very little bother. All she needs is a nice snug, rat-proof box that she can sleep in all winter, and a gentle wash and a touch up to her paint-work in the spring. Incidentally, not only is it absolutely harmless to paint your tortoise's name on its shell (provided you use *non-lead* paint) but it's a good safety measure, too. We've heard awful stories of tortoises who've had garden forks stuck through them, or been muddled up with dead leaves and thrown on bonfires by mistake – just because their camouflage is so good that nobody spotted them. If you put your tortoise's name on in white, non-lead paint, it sticks out a mile and that sort of accident is very unlikely to happen.

We've no idea how old Freda is, but tortoises are one of the longest-lived animals in the world, and it's their beautiful shells that have helped them to survive. They've hardly any natural enemies, and if you can imagine trying to sink your teeth into that tough shell, it's easy to see why! Down at the Crystal Palace Park in London you can get a very good idea of what Freda's prehistoric ancestors looked like. Lurking at the water's edge there are some Dicynodonts, and although they're only painted plaster, they gave me quite a turn when I spotted them peering through the bushes! Dicynodonts lived about 250 million years ago. The name means "double dog tooth" and they're called that because of their two tusk-like teeth. You won't find a tortoise with tusks these days, but there're still plenty around that are just as big. They're the Giant Tortoises and they can weigh up to as much as

Giant Tortoise pictures can be found on stamps. This one's in our Blue Peter Stamp Album.

900 lbs. – which is about 200 times heavier than Freda! Freda is a Greek tortoise and she'll never grow very much bigger, but all the same, it's an odd thought that a tortoise that's only a couple of inches big when it hatches from its egg can one day reach the enormous weight and size of a giant. Mind you, it takes them ten or twenty years to do it, but that's nothing when you remember that these Giant Tortoises can live for anything up to a hundred years. There's even a story that the famous explorer Captain Cook once gave a tortoise to the King of Tonga in the year 1773. And guess when it died? May 19th, 1966! So one tortoise at least lived for 193 years, and who knows, somewhere in the world there may be a tortoise alive now that will have the distinction of being the first to reach 200. I know it's unlikely, but it would be nice to think that tortoise was going to be Freda!

Freda's a fully grown Greek Tortoise.

Giant Tortoises can be as much as 200 times heavier than Freda. London Zoo's Marmaduke tips the scales at five hundredweight.

A Hundred Thousand Presents

The weeks before Christmas are a very busy time, with most people writing out lists of cards and presents for their families and friends. But whatever would you do if you wanted to send presents to a hundred thousand people? It could happen—and it did, more than seventy years ago—to Queen Victoria!

When Queen Victoria was an old lady of nearly 80, and had reigned for more than 60 years, Britain was at war with South Africa—it was called the Boer War.

In 1899, thousands of soldiers were sent to fight far across the sea. They cheered bravely as they went away, leaving anxious families behind them, but when they reached South Africa, they faced great difficulties. The troops had to struggle through dangerous country with their horses and guns. They were forced to fight every inch of their way on exposed land—many soldiers were wounded in the fighting, and many more became ill through the horrible conditions they faced.

Back at home, people were excited when they had news of victories, and sympathised with the hardships the troops were enduring. Some people, though, were against the war altogether; they said the men should be brought home.

In 1899 Britain was at war with South Africa.

Queen Victoria knitted warm clothes for the soldiers.

The Queen wrote an order saying she would give each soldier a Christmas present.

George Cadbury who received the order believed the war was wrong.

The chocolate factory at Bournville, where the presents were made.

Army post offices in South Africa coped with the avalanche of parcels.

Queen Victoria thought about her soldiers a great deal. She wanted the men to know that she sympathised with all they were suffering. She visited hospitals to bring flowers and sympathy to the wounded, and at home, in Buckingham Palace, she knitted busily, making warm clothes for the troops. Soon all the Royal Princesses and Ladies in Waiting joined in. But all the things made at the Palace were given to the officers—the ordinary private soldiers were left without any sign of the Queen's concern for them, and this made Queen Victoria very angry. She thought hard what to do to show that she really cared about *all* her troops, and then she had a good idea. She wrote an order saying she would give every one of her one hundred thousand soldiers a Christmas present—a block of chocolate in a special box.

George Cadbury, the head of one of the country's biggest chocolate factories, received this order. But he believed that war was wrong—that all fighting was wicked, and he was very worried about what to do.

"I must do as the Queen commands," he declared, "because I am her loyal and dutiful subject! But we will not make one penny of profit out of this royal order. I will not make money out of fighting. What is the good of having principles if you are not prepared to suffer for them?"

So his factory at Bournville set to work with a will on the making and packaging of the one hundred thousand blocks of chocolate. A special box was designed, in shiny gold, red and blue, with the Queen's picture, and a message in her handwriting on the lid.

In South Africa, the news was sent to the generals, and soon the army Post Offices were full of sacks and parcels as the presents arrived. The soldiers lined up on parade, very proud that they were each to have a present from their Queen, and back in Britain, Queen Victoria herself gave the boxes to the men who had been sent home wounded. The presents were a tremendous success.

Queen Victoria was delighted. She had shown she really cared about her soldiers, and the presents were a sign of everything she felt.

But little did Queen Victoria know that long after the chocolate was eaten, the boxes would remain precious family treasures. We were lent one by Miss Alice Fairhurst. It belonged to her father, Trooper Fairhurst, who kept it through all the fighting and then brought it home to South London—a little scratched and battered but still a prized possession.

And there are other families in Britain who have similar carefully saved boxes—reminders of the unusual present Queen Victoria gave to her soldiers more than seventy years ago.

MYSTERY PICTURE

Colour the spaces as indicated by the
numbers and the mystery picture will appear

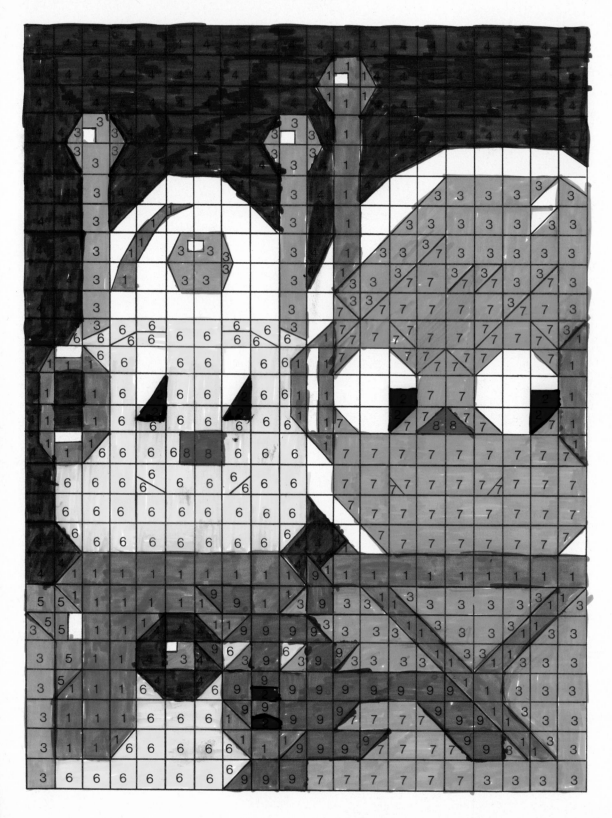

1 Light Blue; 2 Black; 3 Red; 4 Dark Blue; 5 Light
Green; 6 Yellow; 7 Pink; 8 Brown; 9 Dark Green.

MAKE A DOOR STOP

Have you ever wanted to keep a door open ? Most doorstops are expensive, but mine's an old brick in disguise, and it'll keep the heaviest door ajar.

1 All you need, besides your brick, is foam plastic, covering material, glue, and a needle and cotton—and if you've any spare wool, you can decorate the top with a woolly ball kitten.

2 Lay the brick on the foam plastic and draw guide lines. Cut out what you need and stick on to the brick. You can see how I've cut the foam to the exact shape of the brick.

3 The top of your brick will probably have a dip in it—you can feel this through the foam. Lay the brick flat in the middle of the material, dip uppermost.

4 Fold the material neatly round the brick, tucking in all the corners, and sew into place. The seam will not show as it will be the base of the doorstop. You can use the doorstop plain, or add a decoration like the woolly kitten.

5 The kitten is made from five different-sized woolly balls. You can use two or three colours so that it looks like a tabby or a tortoiseshell, or a single colour like this to match your material. Put the woolly balls together in this order. The tail is plaited strands of wool.

6 Fluff the woolly balls and the tail with a wire brush so that they look like fur. Sew them together with matching wool and add felt eyes and ears. The whiskers are strands of wool and the nose a triangle of felt. A ribbon bow and a bell give an attractive finishing touch.

JOURNEY TO YESTERDAY

Once on a glorious summer day, Val and John and I set out on a journey which took us across water and back through time.

The water was the Grand Union Canal which runs from Birmingham to London, and the time was the beginning of the last century. In those days, canals were the only way of getting a heavy load across the country at a reasonable cost. It was also the quickest way, because the railways hadn't been built, and a horse pulling a cart over bumpy, winding roads, had a longer, harder job than the barge horse with a 30-ton cargo gliding behind him on a narrow boat. They were called narrow boats because that's exactly what they are. Ours was seven feet wide and *70 feet* long! The canals were narrow and straight, and the boats were designed to fit them.

For one day only, we were the crew of a beautifully decorated narrow boat, which looked exactly as it had done at the turn of the century.

We had a great, white shire horse called Patience to tow us along, so to complete the score, we dressed up as nineteenth-century boatmen, and set out along a stretch of the old Grand Union. Val, looking every inch a water gipsy, was on the tiller. Johnny was in charge of the ropes, and I was leading Patience who was the only really experienced member of the crew.

We were soon very conscious of our *lack* of experience. At first we thought there wasn't very much to it. After all, you can't very well go the wrong way! But every mile or so, there was a hazard of some kind. We managed to cope without much trouble with a swing bridge, but the locks were a different matter.

The trouble is, there aren't any brakes on a narrow boat, so the only way to stop was to cast off Patience's tow rope, and then loop a restraining rope over a bollard at precisely the right moment. If you cast off too early you have to shove the boat manually, leave it a second too late and you've crashed straight through the top gates of the lock. We built up a routine with Johnny leaping off the boat at the first sight of a lock, and then haring along to be there in time to grab a rope from Val. I think Patch enjoyed this bit more than anybody. He'd stand like a greyhound in the slips waiting for Johnny to jump – and then tear off up the tow path after him, tail wagging, for Val to thrust the rope. Patch really fancied himself as a barge dog. There's a running plank that stretches the length of the hold so that the crew can move quickly from end to end. Patch seemed to think this was built especially for him and patrolled endlessly up and down, like a captain supervising his crew.

We'd had some near disasters at the locks earlier that day. Once, Johnny had to push us ignominiously into a lock with a pole, which would have brought hoots of derision from the narrow boatmen as they queued for the lock in the olden days. On the Grand Union, the locks were meeting places for scores of narrow boat families. When the canal was busy there might have been as many as twenty boats on either side of the lock waiting their turn. They were also the scenes of some bloody fights. The narrow boatmen were tough people, working to a tight schedule. To miss a turn at the lock meant at least half an hour's delay, and fists would fly if someone tried to jump the queue. But today there seemed to be no one on the whole canal but us. I filled Patience's decorated nose can from a fresh water spring, and offered her a drink as the water roared into the lock. When we

We set out along the old Grand Union Canal. Val, looking every inch a water gipsy, was on the tiller.

Narrow boats have no brakes, so to stop, John had to stand by to cast off the tow rope.

The cabin was cleverly designed, not an inch of space wasted. Everything was painted in a beautifully decorative style like a gipsy caravan.

opened the top gates, we had been lifted six feet nine inches and were now 375 feet above sea level at the highest point of the canal. If we'd navigated the Grand Union all the way from London, we'd have been through a total of 94 locks, and with a horse-drawn boat, it would have taken us almost a week.

Whilst I was giving Patience a drink, Val was down below making us a cup of tea.

The narrow boatmen kept their fresh water in a special can. It was always the same neat shape, and always gaily painted, because they took an enormous pride in the appearance of their craft and its equipment. The cabin was beautifully designed, not an inch of space was wasted and everything had its place. The walls were covered with rows of shining horse brasses and souvenir plates from seaside resorts. Every piece of furniture, every pot and pan, and every inch of wall space was painted in a beautiful decorative style – all castles and roses. It reminded us of the decoration on gipsy caravans – but then, people sometimes called narrow boatmen water gipsies.

We'd nearly finished our tea when I spotted what looked like the end of the line. It was the Braunston Tunnel. The tow path came to an abrupt end on the side of a hill; the canal, however, continued through a deep, dark, and seemingly endless tunnel. How do you propel a boat through a tunnel without a horse to pull it? The narrow boatmen had an answer – simple, practical, but desperately primitive. Their solution was to place a board, sticking out on either side, across the front of the boat. Two men called "leggers" would be waiting at the mouth of the tunnel, and, for an agreed sum of money, they would lie back on the plank, place their feet on the side of the tunnel, and "leg" their way through to the other end. There was a little hut by the tunnel where the leggers used to sit and wait for the boats. But unfortunately, the last professional leggers disappeared about 100 years ago, so guess who did the legging for *our* boat?

Whilst we fixed up the legging board, Val unhitched Patience to walk her over the top of the tunnel and (we hoped!) meet us at the other end.

I lay down on the plank and eased myself outwards until my feet touched the dark, slimy wall. My bottom was just overhanging the edge of the plank, so that my balance was preserved by the soles of my feet on the side of the tunnel, and a vice-like grip with my hands on the boat.

"Are you all right, Johnny?" I heard my voice boom down the tunnel.

"You really must be joking," he boomed back.

"One, two, three, go!" I said with no real confidence. Our boots rang out like pistol shots along the length of the tunnel, and every time Patch barked, it sounded like the Hound of the Baskervilles. The important thing was to keep the boat right in the centre of the tunnel so that both of us could reach the walls with our feet.

Val and Patience in the meantime were treading the path which was once worn down by hoof marks, but today was hardly used at all, although it's still known as Boat Horse Walk. Every now and then they came across a great stone air vent which showed Val she was still on the right track.

Meanwhile, down in the tunnel, Johnny and I went slowly and painfully legging our way through, when our panting and scuffling was interrupted by a ghost voice coming from above.

"John – Peter – are you there?" it boomed.

"My gosh – they've come for us!" gasped Johnny.

"Don't be daft, it's Val's voice," I said. "Val – where are you?"

"I'm right on top of you calling down the air vent," her voice echoed all around us like a ghost play on the radio.

At last I saw a tiny circle about the size of a sixpence ahead of us.

"I think we've made it, Johnny," I panted.

Braunston tunnel we discovered after, is 2040 yards long – well over a mile. It had been built entirely by navvies using ordinary hand shovels and picks. I'm glad we didn't have their job. Mind you, at that particular moment, I wasn't all that keen on the one we were doing.

We reached the end of the tunnel and Val was waiting for us with Patience. Soon she had filled the kettle again from the decorated fresh water bucket. It was a lovely summer's day, and the countryside looked just the same as it would have done a hundred and fifty years ago. I felt almost as though we stopped in the Tardis – and just for a day we really *had* been the narrow boat men of 1820.

Although we didn't know it at the time, that glorious day was the last appearance of Patch in a Blue Peter film. That is the way we shall always remember him – inquisitive, full of life and energy, and as always, ready to have a go at anything. He was a great dog!

Navigating the locks was a tricky business. There are 94 of them on the Grand Union Canal.

I filled Patience's nose bag from a fresh water spring and offered her a drink as more water roared into the lock.

I dug my heels into the wooded grooves and heaved the lock gate across the water.

The tow path ended in the side of a hill, but the canal continued through a deep, dark tunnel.

Pete and I lay on the legging board, braced our feet on the tunnel walls and "legged" our way to daylight.

Val, who had walked over the hill with Patience, joined us at the end of the tunnel for a pot of tea.

Poor Horace

This painting of Admiral Lord Nelson hangs in the National Portrait Gallery—one of many reminders of Britain's greatest seaman. Another is Trafalgar Day, October 21st, marking the anniversary of the naval battle fought in 1805 when the ships of the Royal Navy defeated the combined fleets of France and Spain. On this day, Nelson lay dying on board his flagship—shot down by a French marksman—at the very moment of victory. Trafalgar Square in London is named in honour of that battle, and in the centre is Nelson's column. But when you look up and see Admiral Horatio Nelson standing grandly on top, or see portraits of him looking every inch a hero, it's surprising to think that when he was a little boy, even his own family called him "Poor Horace"!

1 "Poor Horace" had seven brothers and sisters—and out of all the children in the Nelson family, he was the delicate one. They all lived at the parsonage at Burnham Thorpe, in Norfolk, where their father was the vicar.

2 The children spent a lot of time playing on the shore a few miles from home, looking out on the bleak North Sea and watching the ships. They had an uncle who was a captain in the Royal Navy, and Horatio made up his mind he would go to sea as well.

3 One day, Captain Suckling was amazed to receive a letter from Nelson's father asking if Nelson could join his ship, *Raisonable*. "Whatever has poor Horace done," he thought, "who is so weak, that he, above all the rest, should be sent to rough it out at sea? But let him come!"

4 The *Raisonable* lay at anchor when Nelson arrived. He felt very young and miserable, and his uncle, Captain Suckling, was not aboard. For the whole of his first day in the Navy, Nelson stood about on deck alone — he was 12 years old!

5 At last, someone showed him where to go — to the midshipmen's mess. The tiny cabin was crowded with ship's guns as well as the midshipmen, and it seemed impossible that they could all live and eat and sleep there for months at a time. But worse was to come.

6 When the ship put to sea, he felt so ill and sick, and deafened by the noise of the wind in the sails that he thought he would never be able to eat or sleep again.

7 But Nelson persevered and worked hard. He studied mathematics and navigation when he was not on duty — for after serving six years at sea, he hoped to be allowed to take the junior lieutenant's examination.

8 It was a gruelling test, but the Admiralty board declared Nelson *had* passed, and then the Chairman broke his silence. He was Nelson's uncle, now Comptroller of the Navy and very grand. "Gentlemen," he said, "permit me to introduce my nephew to you, I knew he would do well without any help from me!"

9 As an officer, Nelson became more and more successful — he was promoted to admiral, but although he was the hero of the Navy and the whole country, he never forgot his early days.

10 Once, years afterwards, the great Admiral Lord Nelson had invited his officers to dinner with him in his cabin. Next to him, according to custom, sat the youngest midshipman — almost too shy to speak. Nelson asked him how old he was. "Eleven years, my lord," said the boy. The great admiral sighed. "It's too young," he said — "it's much too young." For though he was now the Navy's greatest hero,

11 he never forgot his first days at sea, when he was lonely and homesick and everyone called him "Poor Horace"!

Bengo

THREE STORIES
WITHOUT WORDS
by Tim

The Case of the Golden Buddha

Can you solve this case? Six careless mistakes gave away the crooks. We spotted them. Can you?

Bob watched breathlessly as one by one the packing cases were opened. The tension in the little room at the National Museum was almost unbearable. His uncle, Detective Inspector McCann, moved from crate to crate, watching with wary eyes as the Museum staff carefully removed the packing.

This was going to be the biggest Oriental Exhibition ever to be displayed in Britain, and Bob knew that for his uncle, this security job was a very important assignment. He felt very privileged that he'd been allowed to witness the preparations for this extraordinary event. For his special project this term, he was collecting material on Oriental religions, and to be an eyewitness to the unpacking of some of the most famous and valuable treasures from the temples of Ceylon was the experience of a lifetime. He felt privileged, too, to be

watching two of the world's leading Orientalists at work – Sir George Agrot of the National Museum and the strange figure of the Buddhist monk Yoni Addas who had made the two thousand mile flight personally from Ceylon, bearing the smallest, yet most beautiful exhibit of all – the priceless Yellow Buddha of Ceylon. At the moment, Bob could see that he was still clutching the iron-bound box containing the treasure, and since he'd arrived that morning, Yoni Addas had never put it down for a single second. Now the moment had arrived. The monk placed the box on the table and the security men began, slowly and carefully, to prise open the lid. One by one, the sections came away – then as the protective padding was removed, Bob saw the glint of gold and the flash of the jewelled eye.

Sir George stepped eagerly forward. He stretched

out his hand to touch the priceless statuette, and as he did so, the colour drained from his lips. Ashen faced, he turned to McCann.

"Inspector," he gasped, "something's wrong. I'm sure this is not the Yellow Buddha of Ceylon."

"But that is impossible," cried Yoni Addas. "My Lord Abbot himself gave the Buddha into my hands and it has been in my possession ever since. I arrived last night at London Airport. The box has never left my sight!"

Sir George clicked his fingers at one of his staff. "Pass me a knife," he snapped. As he scraped the surface, the blade sliced through the gold and revealed it for what it was – a cheap metal imitation, thinly layered with gold leaf. Shocked, Yoni Addas stepped forward. "Lend me the knife, Sir George," he said.

He prised out the eye and held it to the light. "Glass," he moaned as he peered at it with an expert eye. "I've sworn to guard the Buddha with my life. It is the most sacred relic of the Islamic faith. How can I have failed in this great task?"

"Don't worry, sir," reassured McCann. "The substitution could have been made before the box ever came into your possession. Let's just run over the facts," he said, taking out his notebook. "First of all, how did the Buddha come into your hands?"

"My Lord Abbot gave it to me himself at the Temple in our capital city of Katmandu, where it has been for the last thousand years."

"Were there any witnesses?" queried McCann.

"Yes. The removal of the Buddha from the temple was a moment of such national importance that Mrs Indira Gandhi, our prime minister, herself was present. Then I went straight to the airport and flew directly to London."

The little monk sank down in distress. "You must excuse me," he murmured faintly. "The journey from Ceylon has exhausted me. It's a big step for a man who leads a life of contemplation to fly all the way from our little island in the Pacific and find himself alone in a foreign country, betrayer of his sacred trust."

Sir George stepped up reassuringly. "You've done all you could, Yoni Addas. No blame attaches to you. The responsibility lies with our British security," and he shot a baleful glance at McCann.

Bob seethed at Sir George's veiled insult to his uncle, but McCann didn't move a muscle.

"Tell me about the jewel," he said. "Exactly what does the real stone look like?"

Yoni Addas pulled himself together and did his best to answer. "It is the most wonderful emerald in Ceylon. Of all the beautiful gem stones mined in our island, this was prized for its magnificent yellow gleam and the beauty of its setting."

"I have heard that the figure itself was superb," said McCann. "Can you give me a description of that, too?"

"Yes," said Yoni. "It was a seated Buddha in contemplation. It was made entirely of gold, and the serenity and beauty of the Lord Buddha's face was revered throughout the Orient."

"Thank you, sir," said McCann. "There's just one other small formality. Do you mind if I inspect your personal baggage?"

Yoni Addas sighed weakly.

"Don't bother the poor fellow now," rasped Sir George. "I know what he needs – a jolly good stiff whisky to pull him round."

Yoni Addas' eyes lit up. "You are most kind, Sir George. Whisky always does me good! As for my belongings, they are very few – only my begging bowl and a spare robe. Search if you wish, but it's scarcely worth your trouble."

"I'll be the judge of that, if you don't mind," said McCann briskly, as he turned out the monk's little hold-all.

"What's that?" cried Bob, as a small piece of paper fluttered to the floor.

"It's of no consequence," said the monk, picking up the paper hurriedly.

"Just a moment," snapped McCann, taking the paper from his gnarled brown hand. "This is a ticket to the left luggage department at London Airport."

"What's so unusual about that?" queried Sir George.

"Nothing unusual about the ticket – but unless I'm very much mistaken, you'll find not only the Yellow Buddha at London Airport, but a mysterious trunk as well!"

Suddenly the little monk leapt for the door, but Bob and his uncle were too quick for him.

"Hold him there, Bob, while I get the handcuffs on him," cried McCann.

"But Inspector," expostulated Sir George. "I don't understand. . . ."

"You will, when you see this, Sir George," replied McCann. He leant forward and ran his hand down the face of the terrified monk, revealing a tell-tale white streak.

Both Sir George and Bob were astounded.

"Why, the man's an impostor," cried Sir George.

"You'll find the real Yoni Addas trussed up in a trunk at the Airport," said McCann.

"How did you know, uncle?" queried Bob in amazement.

"He's made six very foolish mistakes," replied Detective Inspector McCann. "He may not be a real monk, but he's certainly got some nasty habits!"

Did you spot the six mistakes? Check your answers on page 76.

Answers

Puzzle Pictures

1 Ugly but harmless—this **Two-Toed Sloth** hung upside down in the studio eating bananas.

2 This 7 week old **baby Tawny Owl** was hand reared after his nest had been accidentally destroyed.

3 Ringo Starr brought his stainless steel Rolls-Royce table to the studio, and an intriguing game called "Another One".

4 Ossie, the baby ostrich, hatched unexpectedly from an egg brought to Britain from South Africa by Mr Alfred Kennear of Monmouthshire.

5 We had our hands full with the **world's largest Teddy bear**. He was made to raise money for charity on a nationwide tour.

6 Stomu Yamash'ta from Japan played his own composition for percussion on a collection of amazing instruments.

7 A World Record was broken in the Blue Peter Studio when champion **Bantam Weightlifter Precious McKenzie** lifted 429 lbs.

8 The Sultanabad carpet, measuring a thousand square feet, was ordered by Adolf Hitler from Persia in 1939. It took eight weavers, working 12 hours a day, five years to complete.

9 This six foot **Giant Cornish Pasty** was made by Miss Dorothy Holloway for Fowey's Annual Regatta.

10 Lesley's first appearance on Blue Peter on May 15th, 1972, when she taught us all a Go-Go dancing routine.

11 James Bond's Moon Car has a six cylinder, 300 h.p. engine, a huge rotating radar scanner, and massive grab "arms" for collecting rock samples.

12 89 year old Mr Alfie Tabb of Kidderminster, who has made the world's smallest bike—14 cm. high, with wheels 5 cm. in diameter. Mr Tabb is the only person who has been able to ride it.

The Case of the Golden Buddha

1 Buddha is not sacred to the Islamic religion. Islam and Buddhism are two different faiths.

2 Colombo, not Katmandu, is the capital city of Ceylon.

3 Mrs Bandaranaike is the Prime Minister of Ceylon, not Mrs Indira Gandhi, who is the Prime Minister of India.

4 Ceylon is an island in the Indian Ocean, not the Pacific Ocean.

5 Emeralds are green, not yellow.

6 Buddhist monk would never accept a drink of whisky, which would be against his vows.

Acknowledgements

All the photographs in this book were taken by Charles E. Walls with the exception of
Picture No. 4 (page 4) by Western Mail; Tree 1972 (page 7) by Dennis Waugh; Mount Etna (page 9) by Keystone Press; all other Etna pictures (pages 10 & 11) by John Adcock; Starehe photographs (pages 28–31) by Mohinder Dhillon; *Queen Elizabeth* (page 34) by Cunard; Top pictures (page 35) by Radio Times Hulton Picture Library; Sinking ship (page 35) by Camera Press; Treetop picture (page 41), two bottom pictures page 42, top picture & bottom left page 43, by Joan Williams; other pictures on pages 42 & 43 by Grahame Dangerfield; Lapps (pages 44 & 45) by Rosemary Gill with the exception of Reindeer (page 45) by Bruce Coleman, and inside hut (page 45) by John Adcock; The Brontë sisters (page 47) by permission of the National Portrait Gallery; Karl Wallenda (page 58) by The Times; Lesley with Freda (page 61) by Joan Williams; Tortoises (bottom right page 61) by Fox Photos; Photographs pages 62 & 63 by Radio Times Hulton Picture Library with the exception of George Cadbury & The chocolate factory (page 63) by Cadbury Schweppes Ltd. Portrait of Nelson (page 70) by permission of the National Portrait Gallery; Blue Peter team (page 77) by Joan Williams.

A Hundred Thousand Presents and *The Brontës at Haworth* were written by Dorothy Smith; *Frost Fair* and *Poor Horace* were illustrated by Robert Broomfield; *Bleep & Booster, Bengo,* and the *Mystery Picture* by "Tim". *The Case of the Golden Buddha* was illustrated by Bernard Blatch; *Icelandic Birds* by Ian Willis; *R.M.S. Queen Elizabeth* by Geoffrey Wheeler.

Useful Information

The pictures of the Brontë sisters and Nelson can be seen in the National Portrait Gallery, 2 St. Martin's Place, London W.C.2.

The Waterways Museum, Stoke Bruerne, Nr. Towcester, Northants. (Tel. Roade 220).

Haworth Parsonage, Haworth, Keighley, Yorks., is open to the public from 11.00 a.m. to 5.30 p.m. on weekdays, 2.00 to 5.30 p.m. on Sundays.

The Brontë Society, c/o Brontë Parsonage Museum, Haworth, Keighley, Yorks. (Tel. 053-54-2323).

International Sheepdog Society, 33 Victoria Road, Darlington, Co. Durham.

Crystal Palace Monsters, Crystal Palace Park, London S.E.19.

Blue Peter Mini Books:
Book of Television
Book of Teddy's Clothes
Book of Pets
Safari to Morocco
Expedition to Ceylon
Book of Presents
Book of Daniel
Book of Guide Dogs

Blue Peter Royal Safari
Blue Peter Book of Limericks.

Biddy Baxter, Edward Barnes and Rosemary Gill would like to acknowledge the help of Gillian Farnsworth and Margaret Parnell

Designed by George Mayhew